Curriculum
as
Social
Psychoanalysis

Teacher Empowerment and School Reform

Henry A. Giroux & Peter L. McLaren, editors
Department of Educational Leadership
Miami University—Oxford, Ohio

In an age when liberalism and radicalism have come under severe attack, American education faces an unprecedented challenge. The challenge has now moved beyond the search for more humanistic approaches to schooling and the quest for educational equality. Today's challenge is the struggle to rebuild a democratic tradition presently in retreat.

Laboring in a climate of anti-intellectualism and cultural ethnocentrism, educators are witnessing the systematic reduction of pedagogical skills and the disempowerment of the teaching profession; the continuation of privilege for select numbers of students on the basis of race, class, and gender; and the proliferation of corporate management pedagogies and state-mandated curricula that prescribe a narrow and sterile range of literacies and conceptions of what it means to be a citizen.

Under the editorship of Henry A. Giroux and Peter L. McLaren, this series will feature works within the critical educational tradition that define, analyze, and offer solutions to the growing dilemmas facing the nation's teachers and school systems. The series will also feature British and Canadian analyses of current educational conditions.

Curriculum as Social Psychoanalysis

The Significance of Place

edited by
Joe L. Kincheloe
and
William F. Pinar

State University of New York Press

Published by
State University of New York Press, Albany

For information, address State University of New York
Press, State University Plaza, Albany, N.Y., 12246

Library of Congress Cataloging-in-Publication Data

Curriculum as social psychoanalysis : the significance of place /
    edited by Joe L. Kincheloe and William F. Pinar.
        p.   cm. — (SUNY series, teacher empowerment and school
    reform)
    Includes bibliographical references.
    ISBN 0–7914–0477–3 (alk. paper). — ISBN 0–7914–0478–1 (pbk. :
    alk. paper)
    1. Education—Southern States—Curricula. 2. Curriculum planning–
    –Southern States.   3. Southern States—Civilization—Study and
    teaching.   4. Social psychology—Southern States.   I. Kincheloe,
    Joe L.   II. Pinar, William.   III. Series: Teacher empowerment and
    school reform.
    LB1570.C88385   1991
    375'.00975—dc20   90–31584
                                                                            CIP

10 9 8 7 6 5 4 3 2 1

Contents

Acknowledgments

Many thanks to the contributors for their chapters. Thanks to Henry Giroux and Peter McLaren for their excellent work in the Teacher Empowerment and School Reform Series. Priscilla Ross deserves much appreciation for her editing. A special thanks to Shirley Steinberg for her help with the editing and the index.

Introduction

——————————— *Joe L. Kincheloe*
and William F. Pinar

Social psychoanalysis is an adaptation of the work of
the Frankfurt School that seeks deeper reading of the word
and the world. Jurgen Habermas considers Freudian psychoanalysis a model for a critical science, for it is psychoanalysis, he states, which serves as an example of a science
incorporating a systematic process of self-reflection. When
psychoanalysis recognizes the presence of neurotic symp-
toms disruptive of a subject's speech, actions, and nonverbal
behavior, it transcends the procedures of traditional herme-
neutics. The world of surface meanings and appearances has
been bracketed by the psychoanalyst, as he or she attempts
to bring to the patient's consciousness the hidden content
of symbolic expression, that is, the life history that has
been repressed. The meaning or significance of a patient's
actions can only be understood in terms of the latent and
unconscious content that move him or her. Successful interpretations that lead to therapy can be formulated only by
uncovering the salient unconscious factors. Therapy pro-
ceeds by making these unconscious factors known to the
patient *and* understood by the patient.

Habermas sees Freudian psychoanalysis—with its concern with the construction of interpretations—as an epistemological basis for social research, and as an important

1

element in the construction of a philosophy of history. Interpretations in psychoanalysis can only be developed within the framework provided by a general theory of neurosis, for example, Freudian psychology. In a similar vein, the social researcher employing a psychoanalytic theoretical structure develops his or her interpretation in the context of a general theory of society—indeed, critical theorists argue—this is the case with all researchers whether they are conscious of their theoretical assumptions or not. Without such consciousness the inquirer is unaware of the unexamined assumptions, values, and forces that guide his or her social and historical interpretations. Using the general theory of neurosis not as an authoritative guide but as a structural model, the psychoanalyst begins to understand neurosis as the consequence of a series of developments that result in what is called "second nature." Second nature, as described by Freud, refers to that part of the psyche constructed by historical forces. To the individual, it appears both rational and natural. The psychoanalyst reconstructs the life history of the patient; the understanding that emerges serves to deconstruct the once impenetrable second nature.

Critical theory seeks to unravel social constructions in order to achieve movement toward emancipation. Using a reformulated, less economically determined Marxism and insights of psychoanalysis, critical interrogations move beyond traditional social science's attempt to interpret historical actors' accounts of their perceptions of themselves and their realities. The actor accounts must be subjected to critical analysis, for they contain formulations that are deemed to be misunderstood by the actors themselves due to social distortion and repression. Thus, guided by its general social theory, social psychoanalysis seeks to trace the interrelationships between ideology and the development of specific societies (Gibson 1986; Gouldner 1976).

Once such interrelationships are established, the distortions internalized and expressed by individuals can be understood by social actors themselves, and human agency in the making of history can be enhanced. According to Habermas, individuals come to be more than mere objects who passively observe and act out the inevitable execution of historical laws, historical determinism can be transcended. Human beings emerge as active agents who, due to their awareness of historical forces and the effects of such forces on individuals, help shape the future expression of these historical forces. Emphasizing the writings of the early Marx in the formulation of its general social theory, critical theory declines to deemphasize the importance of human intentions and the power of humans as creative, meaning seeking actors. Paulo Freire expresses this faith in the possibility of human agency when he argues that history is not a mythical entity outside of and superior to human beings; it does not capriciously command them from above. Such a fatalistic outlook victimize us. We must, he concludes, see ourselves as the subjects of history even if we cannot totally escape being its objects (Freire 1985).

Social psychoanalysis attempts to subvert the given facts by interrogating them historically. Herbert Marcuse argued that the tendency to make existing social arrangements appear rational and natural (i.e., the process of reification) is the product of forgetting. Remembrance in a psychoanalytic sense can move us toward emancipation by releasing us from suffering and permitting us to experience joy. Remembrance changes the world, he concluded, by moving us toward new forms of revolution that celebrate the aesthetic as well as the psychic health of the free individual (Marcuse 1964; Zinn 1984). As the psychoanalyst attempts to remedy the mystified self-understandings of the analysand, the social psychoanalyst sees myth interrogation as an important step toward social progress. Such labor, just like the effort of the psychoanalyst to help patients confront the actual forces that shaped their psyches, is often undermined by the pervasiveness of reification in modern industrialized societies. The power of second nature on the social level is powerful, for history is frozen and seen as undoubtedly rational. Until free people bracket the myths and conceive of the possibilities offered by emancipation, slim is the possibility of authentic self-direction for the individual and society. The less social and individual self-direction that exists, the more it seems that society is governed by rational and intractable natural laws (Habermas 1970, 1974).

In the same manner that the psychoanalyst observes clues in the everyday language of the analysand that can lead to an understanding of the origins of a patient's pathology, the social psychoanalyst uncovers the historical antecedents in the communication of social actors both past and present (Held 1980; McCarthy 1978). This hidden dimension of meaning describes until then unknown aspects of the process of social and historical change, as it discloses the relations among politics, culture, and language. Language analysis becomes a primary source for social and educational research. Marcuse argued that we must "go beyond" the facts, and acquire critical distance from the language that is commonly used and on the surface appears so innocuous and self-evident.

The Nature of Place

Feelings, Eudora Welty wrote, are bound up in place (Gray 1986). Knowing where one started allows one to understand where he or she is. This relationship between place and feeling is central to curriculum theory's study of place. Place is that which brings the particularistic into focus; a sense of place sharpens our understanding of the individual and the psychic and social forces that direct him or her. Without place our appreciation of such particularistic forces tends to be fuzzy and depersonalized. Indeed, place particularizes and conveys embedded social forces.

Place has occupied an important role in the literary theory of the novel. The essence of the novel has been affiliated with local, present, unspectacular day-to-day human experience. Thus, place is the life-force of fiction, serving as the crossroads of circumstance, the playing field on which drama evolves. The interaction between place and theme can be semiotically perceived—the reader decodes the subtle imprint of place on both the unfolding of theme and the development of character.

This reading of place transcends the theory of the novel and moves into the realm of the historical. As place informs our quest to understand the social world, our attention is adjusted to the concrete, the named, the identified. A novelist or a historian cannot remove a story from a particular place; it would no longer be the same story. So powerful is place, Eudora Welty argued, that a bomb that destroyed all traces of places as we know them, would, as a result, destroy all feelings (Welty 1977). When man stood still and looked around him, Welty tells us, he found a god in that place. Whenever, henceforth, the god spoke it was from that particular place that the voice emanated.

Place often cultivates a genius, literary theorists contend. Welty has stated that the interaction between place and genius is a grand symbiosis, for place serves to focus the eye of genius and bring its gaze to a point. Such an intense focus evokes awareness, clarity, and insight—attributes, Welty noted, which often characterize love. The clarifications of place involve setting the abstract in a way accessible to the reader (Welty 1977).

In fiction, place is used to create an world of appearance—a world essential to the novel's believability. Curriculum theory, likewise, must possess a particularistic social theory, a grounded view of the world in which education takes place. Without such a perspective, curriculum theory operates in isolation, serving to trivialize knowledge, fragmenting it into bits and pieces of memorizable waste, while obscurring the political effects of such a process. Fantasy must touch the ground with one toe, satire must construct a kingdom where certain rules apply, and humor must cultivate a fidelity as well as irreverence to place. Commenting on Faulkner's "Spotted Horses," Welty contends that, while being Faulkner's most humorous story, it is at the same time the most realistic portrait of a Mississippi hamlet one could find. Few people understand how imaginative stories such as "Spotted Horses" are works of precise and pure representation: "They are twice as true as life" (Welty 1977).

This literary concept of place finds an analog in the epistemology of social and educational research. The so-called objective world of that which is researched gains meaning and significance (we might say it is "placed") when informed by a self-aware researcher cognizant of the origins of his or her subjectivities and the forces that shape them. Place is a product of human creativity, Faulkner wrote, fashioned out of words, tropes, codes, conventions, and rituals (Gray 1986). The subjectivity of place informs our understanding of the subjectivity of social research in general. It frees us from the pseudo objectivity of positivism (Giroux 1981) and its obsession with the quantification of the human.

Fiction often moves us to unexplored realms of consciousness, in some cases altered states of consciousness. It is not only the sense of place that sets up the backdrop that allows literary "flights" to work but it is also place that brings us back from imaginary experience, permitting us to find our way home. There is another analogy here with our search for a method of social inquiry. Theoretical speculation moves us to a higher ground—we stand on the mountain with its sweeping vantage point and gaze at the world of human affairs. Our sense of place precludes the possibility that we might get stranded in these higher elevations. Place reminds us that the mountainside is one more place, despite its illusion of inclusivity, even omniscience. The abstract (the sweeping, the general) and the concrete (the focused and particularistic) represent two sides of the same epistemological coin.

Place, Welty speculated, is not simply to be *used* by the fiction writer; place is to be unearthed, discovered as the novelist plies his or her trade. The act of writing is self-reflective; it reveals the connection between self and place. This discovery, she concluded, does not connote that place is something new—it suggests that we are (Welty 1977). Thus, the analyzed sense of place is a window to the *Lebenswelt,* a vehicle to self-knowledge, and a crack in the structure that allows the archeologist of self to discover the etymology of one's research act. Why, as curriculum theorists, were we drawn to a particular topic? What predispositions inform our approach? Sense of place provokes insight into such inquiries.

Welty held the concept of "regional" literature in disdain, terming it a "careless term." Regional writing fails to distinguish, she maintained, between localized raw material of life and the subtle process that transforms this primary data into art (Welty 1977). Welty's insight informs the labor to incorporate the concept of place into educational research. For place to inform the act of inquiry it must be turned inside out; in other words, its essence must be uncovered and understood. The raw material of place must be bracketed in such a way that grants insight into the human condition, historical movement and/or anthropological expression. It was Welty, novelist and literary theoretician of place, who could assess the moral and ethical dimension of place. She could create a context in which the universal was subtly evoked in the clarity of the particular—an ability that might inspire curriculum theorists (Havard 1981).

Place and Curriculum Theory

The distinction between scene and place suggests the power of the latter in understanding curriculum. Scene can be understood as the stage, that particular spot where events "take place." When events take place they are *infused by place*. Indeed, place infuses events with values that transcend their capricious distribution in space. Connection of scene, place, and the values of place allows our passionate beliefs to endure. The endurance of place perpetuates hope, not in the static, conservative sense that romanticizes and mythologizes, but in an emancipatory, hopeful sense that accentuates significance, and tragedy, for irony demands appreciation in any analysis of place. For example, Richard Wright is certainly aware of the tragedy of his Mississippi place and hates and hurts because of it. The new world must be constructed on the pieces of love and the fragments of community that live in the place (MacKethan 1980).

It is only when scene is infused with place that the literary imagination is unleashed. Grounded in place one may experiment and explore in aesthetically pleasing *and* socially insightful ways. With its specific detail and its temporal sensitivity, place glows with portent. The embedded temporality of place helps define it. Place is place only if accompanied by a history. F. J. Hoffman calls place "the present condition of a scene that is modified through its having been inhabited in time." (Hoffman 1967). The historical dimension of place informs theory on a variety of levels. A theory that does not sense its consequences in particular places, and that exists in particular historical moments is impoverished. A theory that fails to question its origins as a manifestation of the power of particular places and times and the discourses they produce is seriously limited. The social landscape of a theory, its scene, must be infused by its connections with particular historical places, with the descriptive detail that identifies them, the personalities that inhabit them, and the historical, materialist, and psychic forces that try to shape them.

The literature and curriculum of place, which is informed by theoretical insight, involves a steady accretion of meaning. A process is set into motion in which particulars evolve into generalities without losing their essences, that is, their status as particulars. In critical historiographical study or critical ethnographic analysis of particular curricular settings, the inquirer labors to disclose the profound in the mundane. The synergism occurs when the rhythms of time and fleeting glimpses of the unconscious are integrated with a knowledge of place to reveal hidden designs. In such a process not only place itself is exposed but also the elusive conversation between place and curriculum theory is audible.

Southern Place

For decades social and cultural historians have claimed that the apogee of southern cultural expression has been its creative literature (Roland 1982). Wayne Urban reports that in a discussion with Maxine Greene concerning his scholarly interest in southern educational history, he was advised not to begin his work without a reading of southern literature.

Greene appreciated the power of the genre and its value in any historical endeavor (Urban 1981). Such advice may be extended to the study of curriculum theory informed by place. Although regional history and regional literature from all locales address place, no region has valued place with the fervor of the South. A focus on the South and southern place particularizes our understanding of the sense of place in general and hopefully serves to highlight our appreciation of the relationship between place and curriculum theory.

In traditional southern literary expression, the sense of place is so pervasive that action in the region's novels cannot be imagined in another context. Southern writers find the germ of place in an often fleeting image, a particular southern shadow, the color of an aura, or an idiosyncratic detail. An overlooked particular of the southern idiom may spark a feeling for place that fashions a novel's theme, the historical monograph's interpretation, or a curriculum's focus. In other words, place builds on these shards; it collects them, juxtaposes them, and integrates them into a montage of related images. Southern literary and historical mentors have used this process to create a literature of place.

Southern literature has portrayed the belief that the present is continually instructed by a living past. To deny the past is to spiritually cripple oneself—it is to destroy the future (Garrett 1981). This concern with history cannot be separated from concern with places; the loss of place precipitates the loss of history. This fear of losing place and history has typified the southern literary genre. Lewis Lawson, for example, characterizes southern fiction as "a catalogue of disintegration." Realizing the psychic consequences of such disintegration, the southern literati cultivated a sense of both personal and regional defeat, an understanding of the tragic (Lawson 1984). Place under attack rendered the concept more pointed in the South, perhaps, than in regions where it has been perceived as more secure. Place has a variegated history in the literature of the South. In the postbellum era, place was co-opted as a tool of the mythmaker, as he defined and preserved the tradition. Here no distance existed between mythology and mind. With the advent of the renaissance, place moved to center stage. In this new context, place was viewed with historical consciousness. Such analysis revealed the human construction of place and the possibility that accompanies such as rejection of naturalness. Also, the renaissance use of place as "fable," that is, its personification as an active participant in the literary work extended the use of place as a vehicle for renewal. Used in this manner, place cannot be separated from the rhetoric and pace of the novel. Indeed, meaning was derived through the active participation of place in the construction of character, theme, plot, and moral. In the post-renaissance era, place has been present but has been engaged in a battle for survival with the forces of modernity. Some southern writers have already buried the sense of place and boldly proclaim that southern life goes on without it. Others refuse to sign the death warrant as they diagnose place as merely comatose sustained by life support systems. Still others are not certain as they seek to redefine latter twentieth century place and the form of renewal it promises in the modern South.

An Epistemology of Place

The exploration of place in a regional context highlights the value that place brings to curriculum theorizing. An understanding of southern place involves the history, literature, and sociology of the South; it also involves a more textured understanding of the southern mind—what we might term a southern epistemology. Not only does the South find itself inhabited by the living presence of a unique history, a peculiar literary tradition, and an unusual set of social relationships but Southerners might also be said to possess a distinctive way of knowing, an epistemology of place.

Southerners tend to be suspicious of deterministic ideas, centering themselves on the notion of individual will. In their politics, religion, and literature, Southerners have tended to see themselves as free moral agents. Exterior or interior forces of which they were not aware or over which they had no control did not, they have believed, determine behavior. Social or psychological theory smelled like determinism to the Southerner and were dismissed, often with hostility. For instance, Zig Ziglar of Yazoo, Mississippi, writes in *See you at the Top* (his textbook used in thousands of schools across the South to "promote patriotism, loyalty, and positive self-concept") that the two men who have caused the greatest harm in world history are Freud and Marx. Both men, Ziglar maintains, promoted ideas which claim that men are slaves to forces beyond their control. Reject Freud and Marx he urges students, accept Jesus Christ, and control your own destiny.

Men and women are responsible for their actions and even for the actions of their ancestors, many Southerners believe. In a region with such a tortured past with its evil and suffering, Southerners have been beset by guilt. This notion of responsibility has driven Southerners to extreme denials of the past or to painful struggles for atonement (Lawson 1984). The southern way to deal with the sins has been to tell stories about them rather than proposing abstract explanations. Southerners have consistently rejected the tendency of continental or "Yankee" intellectuals to value abstraction as reality (Montgomery 1981).

Such a mind-set promotes a political conservatism in Southerners that moves them to reject utopian visions based upon theoretical speculations (Havard 1981). Social programs, which are not grounded on a recognition of the ambiguities of the concrete social world, tend not to be supported by many Southerners. Reform based on theoretical generalization will not work, they argue, and serves merely to hide a form of domination from the top down. Reform is only possible in the realm of the particular, they insist. The southern conception of justice is personal. There is suspicion of those who discuss and claim to act on the basis of "a social conscience."

Indeed, due to these southern epistemological predispositions, sociological ways of thinking have not come easily to

Southerners. At its essence, sociology is a generalizing discipline. The sociologist concentrates on commonalities. Sociology applies abstract theoretical categories to diverse social phenomena in order to disclose the similarities between dissimilar empirical situations. idiosyncrasy is often of little interest. Southerners tend to focus upon the very order of detail that social theorists have often instructed practitioners to ignore. Predictably, a sense of place takes on a special importance to Southerners. Similar "details" are not seen as interchangeable; the Southerner is a locally oriented entity with an emotional attachment to specific places.

Southerners have come to know their world through particularity and place. Such a way of knowing finds itself much more at home with philosophical, historical, and artistic modes of understanding human affairs than with the analytical modes of the behavioral and social sciences. Scientism, the Southerner suspects, reduces nature to fact; the entire process is then mystified by statistical manipulation. This is why Southerners have consistently held fill-in the blank questionnaires suspect. Statistics, they scoff, can be used to prove anything. This disdain has made Southerners resistant to the progress of industrial capitalism with its instrumentally rational separation of means from ends (Wilson 1981). The modern era with its ever-spreading industrialization of the South and its conquest of more and more southern schools with its technocratic education is attempting to correct this "anachronistic" southernism.

A southern sense of place implies an historical awareness that expresses itself in an attachment to the extended family—a localism of the *Gemeinshaft* variety. This southern localism involves a tendency to think of communities as distinct from one another and to prefer one's own. At its best, this predisposition is closely related to sense of place as it sensitizes one to those elements that make a community unique: its natural setting with those places, for example, where one likes to be when the sun sets, the webs of friendship, and those kinship ties that would be impossible to reproduce elsewhere (Reed 1982). Such sensitivities often translate into a preference for the concrete over the abstract that places concern with personal, family, and community relations on a higher level of priority than legal, contractual, and formal bureaucratic conventions. Often, southern politics can promote no thirty second TV impression of a candidate that succeeds better than: "He's a solid family man."

A southern epistemology of place holds implications for understanding the "mind of the South" (Cash 1941). Such a mind might discover truth more easily in a particular locale at a particular time. Essences are revealed to people close to the soil as they associate with their neighbors in proximity to the hills, valleys, and streams known intimately by all (Montgomery 1981). This was the argument of the Nashville Agrarians in the early 1930s when they objected to industrialization on the grounds that it destroyed this sacred quality of southern existence. Implicit in the Agrarian position and the southern ethos of localism is a rejection of secularism and its tendency to obscure the particularity of place. "Placelessness" might the great southern phobia be. Southerners are wary of individuals without place. In the southern oral tradition, the traveling salesman is an exemplar of placelessness, and, as such, he is viewed with suspicion.

The "obdurant particularity" of the southern mind hangs on precariously. It is a particularity that intuitively rejects the ravages of late twentieth century industrial alienation with its standardization, anonymity, and distrust of feeling (Wilson 1981). Intuition plays major role in the southern epistemology. Understanding and insight often come to the Southerner in an immediate and spontaneous way. Principles on which life is based are derived from shared emotion rather than a rational process (Havard 1981). The southern mentality, unlike other forms of Western rationality, has often escaped a dehumanizing logocentrism.

The irony of curriculum as social psychoanalysis is that a southern epistemology holds an intrinsic suspicion of such a generalizing construct. The same mentality, which sees reform possible only in the realm of the particular, is uncomfortable with a grand scheme such as "a critically-grounded social psychoanalysis." When history is subjected to secular theorizing a la Hegel, Marx, or the New Humanists, southern scholar Marion Montgomery writes, "humanity" emerges as a shibboleth that may be employed as a tool for manipulation. "The reality of human life," he continues, " 'is 'deconstructed' by whatever self-proclaimed lords of existence have declared the world a mechanism in need of repair. " This is what happened to the children of the 1960s, Montgomery concludes, as "some of them turned to Marcuse in desparation and with violent consequences." Montgomery's comments illustrate the paradox that we have termed southern epistemology (Montgomery 1981).

To read Montgomery's work is to gain an appreciation of the aesthetics of southern particularity and the sense of place that accompanies it. At the same time, however, it confronts us with the underside of a particularity conceived in isolation from the insight of more general analytical devices. The consequences of this underside of southern epistemology have haunted the region for decades. The southern fury against social theoretical generalization that emerges from a radical particularity often encourages an idea-related xenophobia, a discomfort with the intellectual, and aversion to analysis, and a reluctance to embrace reform and social change (Hobson 1981).

This opposition to social reform, which emerges from the epistemology of particularity, finds its expression in the southern perception of the public and private domains. In their particularity, Southerners fail to perceive the existence of a defined public sphere to which all might be committed. The familial space, the private, expands far beyond its literal dimensions to engulf what is typically understood as public space. Racial integration was met with such hostility because Southerners, immersed in their racism and their lack of a public sense, saw the desegregation of public facilities as an invasion of their parlors.

The public or private question in southern life illustrates well the paradox of the southern epistemology. While radical particularity has slowed the necessary legal correction of institutionalized racism in the region, it has concurrently postponed the evolution of the South into a modern mass society where individuals experience self-estrangement and Kafkaesque manipulation by faceless bureaucrats. This is one manifestation of the reaction against modernity that W. J. Cash labels the "savage ideal" of the South (Cash 1941). The southern perception of the private sphere implies that a face-to-face relationship is a better mode for mediating both individual and social conflicts than is a more abstract and legally institutionalized arrangement (Havard 1981).

The southern epistemology of particularity exhibits itself in the region's religious institutions—especially in southern fundamentalism. The discomfort with theoretical generalization is revealed on the religious terrain in the form of a literal mindedness. Epistemological particularity and fundamentalism find themselves in a reflexive relationship: the impulse of particularity helps determine what aspects of the Christian theological tradition are emphasized; the fundamentalist disposition in turn validates providentially the implicit particularistic, socially atheoretical outlook of the southern believer.

The southern evangelist has hardly been the proponent of sophisticated theology. Southern congregations are accustomed to sermons that are tailor-made for their particular sins (Sentelle 1981). Fingers are pointed, toes are stepped on, and in some cases individuals are singled out for condemnation. The code of southern fundamentalist behavior revolves around a litany of: Thou Shalt Nots. Such a code evokes a concern for individual behavior that tends toward mutual surveillance. The concern of fundamentalist parishioners with one another's "goings-on" is reminiscent of Theodor Adorno's description of authoritarian aggression in his work on the authoritarian personality. Southern fundamentalism, thus, has emphasized the action and feeling portions of Christianity while neglecting thought and theological analysis. Such an emphasis leads fundamentalist preachers to exhort their congregations "to give their hearts to Jesus" without a serious examination of just who Jesus was and might be.

Southern fundamentalist believers see individual salvation as the one way to social amelioration. The critical notion of the interrelationship between individual and society is incomprehensible to them. Humans are independent individuals who are bestowed with the power of free will to choose Jesus or to choose hell. The idea of a socially formed individual is not only theoretically incorrect in the eyes of the southern fundamentalist, but it is also unchristian. The particularistic nature of southern political conservatism is, from the fundamentalist perspective, validated by God Himself. (sic) The social construction of personality is not important to a man or a woman concerned with a particularistic God, who determines their eternal destiny in a socially atheoretical manner on Judgment Day.

A true believer, who was raised in a fundamentalist tradition, with its denial of the role of social theory in the process of understanding an individual's destiny, has learned more than a theological position. This particularistic, socially atheoretical training influences the believer to view texts in general as literal documents. So understood, they do not necessitate analysis and theoretical interpretation. They simply need to be rote-learned, that is, committed to memory. A critically oriented teacher, who values text deconstruction, will experience great frustration with fundamentalist students who have been raised to view texts as literal. The attempt to expose the implicit political assumptions of the curriculum will often be met with a literal minded resistance. Influenced by such an epistemological orientation, southern education has suffered for decades from an anti-intellectual endorsement of surface meanings.

Fundamentalist theology is an obvious place to look for the underside of the southern epistemology of particularity, but examples can be found elsewhere. The reaction of some contemporary southern illuminati to fellow Southerners, who have chosen to criticize the malformations of the homeland, is quite revealing. One well-known example is the widespread condemnation of Mississippi journalist, novelist, and editor Willie Morris, who has attempted to explain the nature of the region's racism and conservatism. Ever mindful of the southern sense of place and the insight it may provide, Morris writes of his boyhood home and of contemporary Mississippi life. His portrayal of the changing nature of southern race relations in *The Courting of Marcus Dupree* is an insightful and sensitive portrayal of the modern South.

Morris' work has evoked accusations of treason against the "southern nation." He has told the northern liberals what they want to hear, George Garret writes. By denouncing southern life Morris and other "traitors" have ingratiated themselves to their northern "oppressors." Morris and his friends, like slaves of the Old South, pull wool over the eyes of the Yankee liberals by:

> acting out with gusto and enthusiasm the part already assigned to them. This example is not likely to be followed by many southern writers, if only because there is no room for more than a few "house Southerners" in the North at one time.[1]

Garrett's brand of conservatism is grounded on a localism turned sour—a localism that has turned into provincialism. Southerners who criticize Willie Morris in this way offer merely a chauvinistic defense of one's locale. Epistemological particularism becomes in this case a means for protecting unjust power relations. The social wounds of southern racism, sexism, and class bias will never be healed by mass amnesia covered by false pride.

Thus, the paradox of the southern epistemology of particularity reflects the larger enigma of the South: Mardi Gras and Jimmy Swaggart, Elvis Presley and Tennessee Ernie Ford, moonshine and Baptist punch, Hunter S. Thompson and James J. Kilpatrick, Andy Griffith (as sheriff of Mayberry), and Bull Conner. Faced with such paradox, Southerners often find generalization vexing. As a result, they have sought an anecdotal mode of particularity—an orientation that has helped produce the southern raconteur. The southern storyteller as cultural figure transcends classification as mere entertainer, for the storytelling becomes a means of comprehending reality, a method of reasoning. Cultural forms in the South often develop from a storytelling impulse. The American South with its epistemology of particularity produced country music. Indeed, country music symbolizes the anecdote as an epistemological form.

The lyrics of country music tell stories that are loaded with details—the journalistic who, what, when, where, and why (Reed 1982). Country singers are not dealing with Everyman but with particular people from particular southern places: Blue Ridge Mountain Boy, Louisiana Woman, Mississippi Man, Blue Kentucky Girl, and so forth. The stories of Johnny Cash and Tom T. Hall tell us of the locales, the predispositions, the appearances, the "mud, the blood, and the beer" of their subjects. When Johnny Paycheck sings "Take This Job and Shove It," we do not listen to a treatise on worker-management conflict but a story about a particular worker and a particular foreman with a flattop haircut. In "Wreck on the Highway" Roy Acuff sings of a car crash in such detail that his descriptions of whiskey and blood running together invite satire of the song as camp comedy. Whatever our reactions, the songs share the emphasis on the particularistic so characteristic of the South. The emphasis on the individual, the concern with locale, the literary sense of place are all manifestations of the southern epistemology of place and particularity. To understand the South and its history, to deconstruct the codes of the region, and to develop the southern curriculum, one must be familiar with this peculiar and paradoxical view of the world.

Toward a Curriculum Theory of Place

Any analysis of curriculum theorizing must confront the nature of social theory and its relationship to the study of curriculum. Before we proceed farther in our effort to link theoretically social psychoanalysis and the concept of place, an examination of the nature of social theory is necessary. When social phenomena have to be explained, social theory is commonly invoked to postulate certain structural patterns that provide a causal interpretation of the regularities in those phenomena (Jaggar 1983). The employment of social theories or the study of curriculum over the last fifteen or twenty years has dramatically influenced the field, transcending the naive perspectives of the traditionalists and the empiricists who used to dominate the field (Giroux, Penna, Pinar 1981). When social theory confronted curriculum, the field's inescapably political character was exposed; the relationship between economic structure and the study of education was revealed; the mystifications of bourgeois individualism that denied the interplay between individual and social relationships were uncovered; and the importance of social vision and commitment for both theorist and practitioner to social and economic justice was realized. Indeed, the contributions of social theory have been remarkable. If curricularists are to continue to progress, to further develop theory, and to catch the "second wave" of reconceptualization—the praxiological dimension of our theorizing in elementary and secondary schools (Pinar 1988; Dugas and Edwards 1988)—we might link the particularistic with the general.

Suggestive of such work is that of Henry Giroux and Peter McLaren who have used critical social theory to examine the underlying political and economic foundation of the larger society and their relationship to specific curriculum issues (Giroux 1983; Giroux 1988; McLaren 1989). To understand the significance of social facts, Henry Giroux writes, one must understand those larger structures of the larger society. Such understandings constitute the essence of the value of social theory: It provides the key to the historical situation in which one finds himself or herself (Giroux 1983). When one adds the insight provided by an examination of the Greek root of the word theory, *theoros* (to watch a spectacle), then cognizance of historical situatedness can be dialectically linked to the insight derived from concrete situatedness, that is, place. The value of individual experience is thus linked particularistically and historically.

The critical spirit of the social theory Giroux and McLaren have brought to curriculum has performed a significant unmasking function in its refusal to confuse appearance and essence. Theodor Adorno maintained that theory must transform the concept that the object it confronts has of itself. Upon removing socially imposed concepts from the object, it must elicit what the object seeks to be. What it seeks to be must be confronted with what it is. Thus, the object finds itself in a dialectical tension between the reality of how it has been socially formed and the possibility of what it could become (Giroux 1983). Critical students of curriculum must refuse to take such conventions seriously; rather, students must subject them constantly to the analysis of what could be. When the conventions, the codes, the shibboleths of a field are approached with a deferential reverence, no truth is to be uncovered.

Critical social theories begin with an examination of the relationships that exist between the part and the whole, the specific and the general. Individual human beings operate in this dialectical context as they create and are created by their social world (McLaren 1989). The juxtaposition of social psychoanalysis and place acknowledges this critical theoretical construct; such a juxtaposition attempts to acknowledge its debt to critical theory while extending the political unmasking function through the study of particularistic.

A empiricist-positivist model of theorizing is trapped in the pseudo-neutrality of classifying and ordering because it failed to develop the capacity for meta-theory. A positivistic social theory is blind to both the so-called objective interests it represents and the historical development of these interests. Without the illumination of meta-theorizing, positivistic analysts fail to recognize the various ways their interests will limit their insight within specific historical contexts. Theory is always affected by the historical moment and the *Zeitgeist* in which it is applied. The relationship, however, is dialectical: Theory is not reducible to its context (Giroux 1983). The analysis of the work of theoreticians, that is, their moment in history, their class, their place in the world, their interest in their world, and their consciousness of their place and interest can inform the act of theorizing.

Curriculum theory cannot advance if it abstracts itself from time, history, place, and human intention. Social and curriculum theorists must direct themselves to history (including their own histories) as a *whole*—not merely to the political-economic dimensions of the past, or the psychological underpinnings of tradition, or to a parade of "great men" (*sic*). Knowledge is skewed when it fails to account for the realities of particularity or collectivity. The field of psychology, for example, tends by its very nature to be focused on the individual and the particularistic. Patterns of behavior, syndromes began to emerge as experts systematically studied the human mind and behavior. Theories were developed to account for what was observed. However, like other disciplines, psychology finds itself existing in particular places in specific historical moments (Kovel 1981). Without an understanding of the generalizing notions of social theory, psychology can find itself unconscious of its own binding by time and context as it attempts to explore consciousness itself. The naive explanations of personality formation, which have come out of that discipline, illustrate the significance of the epistemological synthesis we seek.

The appreciation of individual sensation can be the genesis of larger political awareness—the refusal to deny restlessness, discomfort, moral ambiguity, and the impulse to reject. As one struggles with the problematic nature of the lived world, he or she begins to sense the unity of self and situation. Eudora Welty understood this struggle when she wrote that "our knowledge depends on the living relationship between what we see going on and ourselves" (Mac-Kethan 1980). This is a rationale for autobiography in curriculum studies. Autobiography can confront the meaning of the given world, reject it, reformulate it, and reconstruct it with a social vision that is authentically the individual's.

Place becomes an important means of linking particularity to the social concerns of curriculum theory. A sense of place allows for an intensified focus on sensation. Such a focus provides a sense of direction and identity that might empower individuals to struggle and to endure. Informed by place, this act of focusing can hold an intrinsic beauty and meaning that intensifies as it matures, emerging as poetry and politics (Huebner 1975). Like a form of phenomenological bracketing, such focusing assumes the role of seer, revealing insight to those who can stand still long enough to catch the moment—the instance when the particularity of place reveals that which is contained in sensation.

Such contemplations may be suggested by Joel Kovel's concept of "totality" (Kovel 1981). Totality implies a notion that is broader than either particularity or a generalized socioeconomic pattern; however, it encompasses them both. Human beings are entwined in countless ways in this totality, which in the particularistic domain, involves place and individual consciousness, while in the generalized realm includes psychological, social, political, and economic patterns. In light of Kovel's totality both politico-economic and individual-focused curriculum theorists might reunite. Totality implies radical reconceptualization as well as radical action.

Totality connotes an understanding of the individual in relation to history—history in all its multidimensionality. As a discipline, which lends itself to historical study and through that study transformation, curriculum theory must view history in the context of totality. History so viewed is simply neither a linear story of social, economic, and political forces, nor is it a series of particularistic anecdotes; history as totality involves an examination of both and an appreciation of the dialectical interplay between them. Knowing in the historical sense is not the exclusive domain of "experts" isolated from the "lived world." However, our examination of that which passes as knowledge in our educational institutions suggests an ignorance of such a disclaimer.

An epistemological synthesis viewed as totality precludes any sense of certainty that immunizes theory from those reassessments that lived experience necessitates. Any social theory that regards the particularistic, or the personal as a derivative category is imprisoned in a cell of its own creation. An ossified Marxism, for example, which disregarded the particularistic was unable to account for the conservatism of the proletariat. The Frankfurt School had to explain the social and psychological forces that worked in concert to move working people to act in a manner contrary to their own interests. In the process, the critical theorists argued that the control of the means of production was not a sufficient condition for liberation. Indeed, the essence of liberation is attached to the notion of totality, of epistemological synthesis. We invite you to explore these ideas in the essays that follow.

Part I

Historical and Political Elements

1

Farragut School: A Case Study of Southern Progressivism in the Upper South

Clinton B. Allison

Introduction

The unifying theme of this book is place. But the South is not a place; it is many places. This chapter is a case study of a particular school in a particular place in the upper South—Farragut School in rural Knox County, Tennessee, at the beginning of the twentieth century. Farragut was in the South, but a different South from Susan Huddleston Edgerton's Ruston, Louisiana, or Joe Newman's Mobile, Alabama. Such common (and rich) themes in the history and literature of southern society as the complex, often steamy relationship between "artistocratic" white Southerners, Blacks, and poor Whites is largely absent in this South. Rather, East Tennessee was a South of small farms, isolated by valleys and ridges, a region that sent more of its sons to the Union than to the Confederacy in what Southerners still prefer to call the "War Between the States." The population was overwhelmingly White, chiefly English and Scotch-Irish. (But, in a case study, anomalies provide texture and temper generalizations, for one of the leading families in this story was German Amish.) It was a region of so few Blacks that they were often a curiosity for isolated farm families, who came into contact with them only during their occasional visits to Knoxville.

But Southerness is both place and state of mind. And the residents of East Tennessee matter-of-factly considered themselves Southerners. Some of their ancestors may have worn the blue rather than the gray, but they shared in the Southerners' "group identification," which Joe Kincheloe mentions elsewhere in this book.

The Farragut community today is the most prosperous and cosmopolitan suburb of Knoxville. There are more "outsiders" here (and in nearby Oak Ridge) than elsewhere in East Tennessee. But for the most part, the people of the area remain self-consciously southern: they feel at home in visits to Alabama and Georgia, but Ohio (except among the pockets of Appalachians in Cincinnati and Cleveland) represents an alien culture. A few miles to the southeast of Farragut in Gatlinburg, the most popular resort town of the upper South, tourist items from rugs to T-shirts include the admonition: "If your heart ain't in Dixie get your ass out." About the same distance to the northwest of Farragut at Clinton, the White Citizens Council led one of the most publicized and meanspirited confrontations against school integration in 1956.[1]

Farragut School was created by the southern progressives in 1903 as a model rural school for the South, and this chapter is a case study in southern progressivism. In the first decade of the twentieth century, educational campaigns led by southern reform-minded college presidents, professors, and mainline Protestant ministers (and financed by northern capitalists) propagandized for free, tax supported schools in each of the southern states. The Southern Education Board and the General Education Board were created to administer the campaigns and to solicit money from Yankee captains of industry and merchandising. The Southern Education Board hired agents to campaign for public schools in each of the southern states and established a bureau of information and investigation in Knoxville.

The primary purpose of the educational campaigns was much the same as that of the common school crusade of a

half-century before in the North. One of the leaders, Edwin
A. Alderman, president of Tulane, promised in 1902 that
"this educational crusade shall not cease until every
child . . . high or low, White or Black, bond or free, shall be
emancipated from the great, Black empire of ignorance and
of night."[2] But, as in the earlier campaign, literacy was secondary to character education. The Right Reverend Davis
Sessums assured his fellow reformers that they were not interested in "any worship of mere brain culture apart from
the development of manhood and character."[3] The progressive agenda also included efficiency, particularly in school
administration; school consolidation; the school as a "community center"; the use of survey to determine community
"needs"; and, most important for this case study, an agricultural and industrial curriculum.

In his chapter, William Pinar comments that "the concept of public domain remains underdeveloped in the South."
The southern progressives battled this lack of sense of responsibility on the part of Southerners of all classes to support public schools. The reformers blamed the carpetbaggers
and scalawags of the reconstruction period for exaccerbating
the negative attitudes of Southerners toward tax dollars for
public purposes; they had given expenditures for public
schooling a Yankee stain that had to be cleansed if Southerners were to be convinced that they should tax themselves
to provide adequate schooling for their young. The northern
philanthropists, who bankrolled the activities of the southern progressives, were careful to assure Southerners that
they were not a new generation of carpetbaggers; they were
much more enlightened. They were careful to stay in the
background, allowing "native" Southerners to make procla-
mations about educational needs and to manage the political campaigns.

Among the prominent southern leaders of the campaign
were the president and the head of the department of education at the University of Tennessee. They were also instrumental in the creation of Farragut School. The University
was deeply involved in the southern educational campaigns
of the time, and it was doing well by doing good. President

Charles W. Dabney, with a patrician Virginia background, got on well with the philanthropists who were financing the movement; he was determined to make his University head-quarters for the campaigns. The Southern Education Board established its bureau of information and investigation in Knoxville, and the propaganda journal of the campaigns, *Southern Education,* was published there. A new depart-ment of education, modeled after Columbia's Teachers College, was financed in large part by the General Education Board, which also gave most of the monetary support for the ambitious Summer School of the South.[4] Philander P. Claxton, a native Tennessean and alumnus of the University, was brought in by Dabney to administer these programs. Ambitious, handsome, and vain, Claxton was a true believing cru-sader, who was as adept as Dabney in getting his hands in the pockets of John D. Rockefeller, Jr., George Foster Peabody, Robert Ogden, and other northern supporters of southern education.[5]

In 1902, Georgia's Hoke Smith called the leaders of the southern educational progressives "big-hearted patriotic philanthropists."[6] A speaker before the Conference for Education in the South described them as "men and women of culture, of wide experience, broad views devoid of selfish-ness, and hearts beating with sympathy for the needs of their fellowmen."[7] Traditionally, educational historians have agreed with this assessment. Charles W. Dabney's two vol-ume historical apology of the movement, *Universal Educa-tion in the South,* overflows with hyperbolic praise of the reformers and their ideas.[8]

But as Kincheloe and Pinar observe elsewhere in this book, "when the conventions, the codes, the shibboleths of a field are approached with a deferential reverence, no truth is to be uncovered." Revisionist historians have more criti-cally reinterpreted the work of the southern educational progressives, finding social control as the motivation for the use of the schools as community centers and for the stress on teaching traditional values. Administrative efficiency, school consolidation, and school surveys have been criticized as techniques for substituting professional and elite control over schools at the expense of democratic localism. And agricultural and industrial curricula have been characterized as class and race biased because they attempted to prepare disadvantaged Blacks and underclass Whites for roles at the bottom of the social structure.[9] The revisionist critique informs the case study that follows.

Farragut Today

Farragut, an incorporated town of 11,000, butts squarely against the west side of Knoxville, Tennessee. Robert S. Cotterill, in his 1948 presidential address before the Southern Historical Association, argued that "there is, in very fact, no Old South and no New. There is only, The South. Fundamentally, as it was in the beginning it is now, and, if God please, it shall be evermore."[10] Forty years later, it seems that such continuity has not pleased God, at least in the surburbia of the upper South. Because Farragut today could be almost any place in suburban America; it is the same familiar yet bizarre tangle of fast food chains, automobile dealers, smart little shops, and developers devouring the last of the farmland with new "communities," each one with more expensive houses than the last. But, because this is the South, the houses are likely to be traditional in style, sham Georgian or pretend turn of the century farmhouses. But farmhouses that few southern dirt farmers could ever have afforded and with "amenities" they could not have imagined—mud rooms and dressing rooms, hot tubs and jacuzzis, electronic rooms for couch potatoes, and lord knows what all. Much of the population is transient but also affluent: corporation executives, university administrators, Oak Ridge scientists. Certainly there are more upper middle-class Asians and Blacks than is typical of East Tennessee. Many of the parents work for multinational corporation, and their children travel the world, with or without their parents. According to the curriculum principal of Farragut High School, students often travel in groups or pairs without adult supervision, sometimes arriving "late to school in September

because they have just returned from Asia or other countries
[sic] around the world."[11]

Members of the Farragut community consider their
high school to be exemplary. So do many who live outside
the school district; parents from as far as one hundred miles
away have been known to rent apartments or buy condomin-
iums in the district for their adolescents so that they can
attend Farragut. The school reflects the world of its patrons
in that it is structured and administered like a multinational corporation. Efficiency, science, innovation, favorable
publicity, administration by team management, and a diversity of viewpoints are emphasized. The curriculum is academic and college preparatory. The students are placed in a
hierarchically tracked system of academic programs. Nearly
15 percent of the students are in the honors track and an
additional 71.4 percent are in the college preparatory
track.[12]

Lamar Alexander, the state's "education governor," described Farragut as "an excellent example of a first rate
school in a first rate system."[13] In 1983, when President
Reagan was making the quality of public schools a political
issue, Farragut was the first public school he visited. David
Rockefeller dropped by and presented a $10,000 Rockefeller
Brothers Foundation award for outstanding programs in the
arts. Farragut could have been a model for former Education Secretary William Bennett's ideal high school, James
Madison High School.

Farragut Historically

Throughout its history Farragut has been an exemplary
school. It was created in 1903 as a model rural school for the
South. The Rockefeller endowed General Education Board
helped to finance the first building, the Southern Education
Board sponsored its development and nurtured its early
years, and it served as a demonstration school for teachers
from throughout the region who attended the Summer
School of the South at the University of Tennessee. In 1913,

United States Bureau of Education Bulletin No. 49 ("The Farragut School: A Tennessee Country-Life High School") was devoted to Farragut. The School won a silver medal as a model rural school at the Panama-Pacific Exposition in San Francisco, and, in 1917, it became the nation's first Smith-Hughes Agricultural School.

This historical study is based on the premise that we can learn something of consequence about public schooling in the South from a close examination of one school over time. Farragut School was not chosen for the study because it is an extraordinary school (although it obviously is), but because it reflects so well many of the changes that have taken place in southern society and schooling in the twentieth century.

The first decade of Farragut School is instructive about southern progressives. The school was their creation, and they, perhaps more than progressives generally, struggled with ambivalence towards modernization and nostalgia, between embracing the technology of the future, and despair for the loss of the virtues of the past, even if an imagined past. Their romantic attachment to a belief in a relationship between goodness and agrarianism was fundamental. The roots were well established in the southern soil of Jeffersonism, but the new New Yorker, roughriding president, Theodore Roosevelt, was helping to nurture a national impulse, which would soon spring into a national country life movement.[14] Roosevelt and many of the progressives were not only afraid of race suicide because of uncouth new immigrants, but they also feared the degeneration of the national character by coming generations of city dwellers who had not experienced the moral instruction inherent in living close to God's nature. The solution was to use technology to make living on the farm more attractive. Modern machines and methods could take the drudgery out of the lives of the farmer and his wife and make them more prosperous. Better roads and free rural mail delivery and telephones would help end their isolation. And more attractive farm housing (including indoor plumbing) and flower gardens would alleviate their aesthetic deprivation.

The standard story of the origins of Farragut School exemplifies traditional southern progressive historiography. In
1903, when the school was being organized, the surrounding
community was rural and isolated. Concord, the site, was
not really a village, just a few scattered stores among corn,
hog, and dairy farms. The community was connected to
Knoxville by fifteen miles of the unpaved and often muddy
Dixie Lee Highway. In this poor, southern community, farmers were concerned about their youth forsaking the barren,
isolated, and otherwise unattractive life of the farmer for
the lure of riches and the excitement of cities. They wanted
to make farming more prosperous, to provide more beauty in
their rural environment, and to enhance the social life of
farm families, not only for future generations but also for
their own wives and children. Sharing a widespread American faith in education, they banded together and approached
professors of education at the state university, who decided
that they needed a scientific community survey (a common
ploy of the progressives to convince communities that they
needed what progressive educators wanted them to have).

   The survey indicated the need for an agricultural high
school. The farmers organized a political campaign and gar-
nered almost unanimous support for such a school. Armed
with evidence of widespread community support for such a
noble undertaking, Charles W. Dabney, president of the University and Philander P. Claxton, head of the department of
education, convinced the Southern Education Board to endorse the project. The closely allied General Education
Board generously paid half of the cost of building the school,
with the understanding that it would be a model rural
school for the whole South as well as teachers, who were
attending the Summer School of the South (also conducted
by the Southern Education Board and financed by the General Education Board).

   A closer examination of the school's origins reveals a
more complicated story, which can add to an understanding
of issues of power, class, and gender in southern progressivism. First, there is the issue of power: Who controlled the
aims, curriculum and administration of the school? I argue

that effective power was exercised by a coalition of wealthier farm families and a group of administrators at the state university with close ties to northern philanthropists. The Stoltzfus family played the most prominent role in the establishment of the school. Of German Amish extraction, they had been in the community since 1868. The patriarch, C. H. Stoltzfus, was the "prime mover" in establishing the school. He proposed it, chaired the committee that organized the campaign, and was one of ten farmers who pledged $200 each to construct the building.[15] He was by no means a poor farmer. He and his brothers were owners of Sunnyside Farms, one of the largest dairies in the area. In 1902, Wallace Buttrick, executive secretary of the General Education Board, visited "Farmer Stoltzfus," observing that he had "one of the best farms in the South."[16]

The relationship between Stoltzfus and Claxton was not the result of a serendipitous encounter between an education-oriented farmer and the head of the Education Department at the University. One of Stoltzfus' daughters was married to Claxton's colleague, C. E. Ferris, the University's well-known professor of chemistry. Claxton had worked closely with another daughter, Amanda, principal of Girls High School, Knoxville. She was a graduate student at Teachers College, Columbia and a faculty member in the Summer School of the South. And, in what must have been a lucrative contract, Sunnyside Farms supplied dairy products to the Summer School of the South. Finally, Amanda soon became principal of Farragut.

Although the school was "open to all White children" in the school district from the beginning, upper middle-class families remained its chief clients. The 1913 United States Bureau of Education Bulletin on the school contains a photograph with a caption that explains that it shows a group of farmers at a school meeting "to discuss canning factories and corn growing." The men, women, and children are all stylishly dressed, with the prosperous looking men in three-piece suits, and, in several cases, highly shined shoes. It is about as unlikely a group of typical East Tennessee farmers as can be imagined.[17]

The establishment of a modern rural school for southern communities was just the sort of thing that the philanthropists could be expected to fund. Dabney explained the vision of the school to an applicant for a teaching job there in 1903:

> The school is visited by hundreds of superintendents and teachers from all parts of the South, and if only its plans can be well carried out, it will exert a tremendous influence in molding the new rural school of the South. It is, in brief, a practical experience in the new education, adapted to the needs of a southern rural community.[18]

Indeed, the letterhead on the stationery of the new school was: A MODEL RURAL SCHOOL.

Claxton and Dabney worked closely with Stoltzfus in organizing and funding the school. They attended the community meetings of "large and representative crowd[s] of citizens" to campaign for the school.[19] They, and a good part of the faculty of the Summer School of the South, were present in July, 1903 when the cornerstone was laid for the school with much speechmaking.[20] Official control over the school was somewhat ambiguous until it became part of the county school system in 1906–07. But Dabney claimed that Claxton was "immediately in charge" and that it was "connected" with the department of education where it had "the benefit of the advice and the direction of its professors."[21]

The administration of Farragut School and the education faculty in the University of Tennessee had an open, unembarrassed dependency on northern philanthropists. They behaved as if the philanthropists had a moral obligation to support southern schooling. There was a kind of philanthropic dependency, not unlike the welfare dependency that conservatives of another generation complain about. There was a continuing flow of letters requesting funds from contacts in the north. Claxton had a longtime correspondence with Mari Hofer, of Teachers College, and he tied to appeal to her to solicit support from her New York liberal acquaintances who wished to improve life for poor Southerners: "The school also has a poultry yard and is attempting to show the people the best methods of growing poultry for profit," he wrote. "In other words," he continued, "we are trying to make a model country school in which the subjects of most interest to country people will be united with general culture subjects."[22] Amanda Stoltzfus wanted more books and materials on crafts for the Farragut School Library. She argued that Andrew Carnegie should help. "Surely," she wrote, he "would be interested in a little section of his own country which is struggling to give its children a plain education that will aid in making them better men and women—better citizens. . . . He has helped negroes [sic], why not his own race?"[23]

When the school building burned in 1906, Principal Stoltzfus and her supporters at the University looked to the North for help. Dabney, now president of the University of Cincinnati, promised to write to "one or two persons," but insisted that Stoltzfus contact the Southern and General Education Boards: " . . . they certainly know of your good work and will be glad to consider an application you make. I should think the General Education Board would be willing to help you a little again,"[24] Dabney assured her. Stoltzfus was outraged when the General Education Board (GEB) refused further support: "I cannot see for my life why northern people who have money to devote to philanthropic purposes, [sic] do not see the greatest field in just such causes as our school represents. The teachers and our people have made sacrifices which surely proves the faith they have in the work, and the addition of a few thousand dollars would again put us on our feet where we can hope to move toward our ideal—a model rural school."[25]

Schooling and Community

Control over the school was in the hands of outsiders and the wealthy in the community. They also left the historical record; thus, the level of support for the school among the common folk cannot be precisely measured. As usual, particularly in the South, the voices of the rural poor can be heard only faintly by the historian.

A theme of revisionist historians has been that the progressive policy of school consolidation threatened a sense of community and the democratic localism that existed in district schools. The apologists for Farragut argued the opposite. Several small schools had been consolidated to form Farragut, leading to a sense of community rather than away from it, according to the school supporters. Farragut became a community center in the best progressive sense. The school catalog stressed this idea: "One of the things in which rural life is preeminently lacking is sociability. The farmers do not get together in a social way as they should. . . . We try to make our high school the social and intellectual center of the community."[26] "Occasionally," wrote a columnist for the local newspaper, "a mountaineer and his wife will come down from the hills, 20, 30, 40 miles away, and spend a week or a month at this school. . . . "[27] The visitors provided extra income to local farmers by boarding with them. Indeed, it was said to be such a model that "the endeavor all over the state was to do away with the little red schoolhouses and its [sic] lonely teacher" by consolidation.[28]

The picture painted in contemporary accounts was agrarian romantic. School days were devoted to community socials with "spelling bees, debates, cooking classes and much good cheer with the help of hickory nuts, apples, and popcorn."[29] The biggest celebration of the year was commencement day. The program lasted all day starting with talks and essays by graduating seniors, "usually upon subjects pertaining to farm and country life." A basket dinner was served under the shade trees on the grounds at noon; then there was inspection of the school fields, which were to be an object lesson in the virtues of crop rotation. The commencement address by a "prominent outside speaker" followed. Then the high school baseball team played a team of local farmers. Finally, in the evening, the students presented a drama to what must have been an exhausted audience of families and neighbors.[30]

School baths and the library were available to members of the community and remained open in the summer. Farragut was the first school in East Tennessee to have indoor plumbing, which included showers with hot water: "applicants are merely expected to bring their own soap and towels."[31] Revisionist historians have been suspicious of school baths, saying that they were part of the progressives' agenda for public schools and thus should be critically examined as examples of imposition, social control, middle-class bias, or, at the very least, confusion about what should be the aims of public schools. There is no hint of complaints from farm families in the Farragut community, who commonly lacked indoor plumbing.

In the first decade of its existence, there was no community opposition voiced in any newspaper or other public account to any aspect of Farragut School. But the private correspondence of Dabney, Claxton, and the Farragut faculty tell a different, if vague, story. A few examples will suffice. "Have the people stopped quarreling and do they support you well?" Dabney asked Samuel Chesnutt, Farragut teacher, in 1905[32] Chesnutt responded that generally the school was "getting along very well. Contention and opposition is gradually dying out."[33] But, less than six months later, under mysterious circumstances, the school burned. Principal Stoltzfus was optimistic about the future: "The fire seems to have left a bond of sympathy where before was discord and opposition."[34] The nature of the opposition cannot be determined from extant documents; the proponents of the school kept the paper.

The Agricultural Curriculum

Although issues related to consolidation and control may be suspected as sources of opposition, there are also suggestions of controversies over curriculum. A problem in any historical discussion of curriculum is to determine what the curriculum actually was rather than what was claimed—because it was thought to be desirable or politically expedient. This problem is exaccerbated when outside funding agencies support a school because it has the "correct" curriculum as was the case with Farragut.

Farragut claimed an agricultural curriculum. According to the 1911 catalog 90 percent of the students took the agricultural course of study.[35] Lectures were given "on farming, housekeeping, cooking, dairying [remember that Stoltzfus ran a large dairy], dressmaking." But, much in keeping with the southern progressives generally, students were also taught the proper values: To be "polite, active, thrifty, energetic, leanly[?], healthy."[36] The methods reflected broader progressivism: "The idea here is not so much to crowd the minds with facts but to create an interest in the wonderful things of nature relative to farming."[37] A contemporary journalist approvingly called the school "a kindergarten for higher grades."[38]

Yet there was a bias in favor of a traditional, college preparatory curriculum. The 1906 catalog emphasized the agricultural course of study, including horticulture, domestic science, and manual training, but commented that at the same time "the more ambitious student was to be prepared for college."[39] Occasionally the supporters of the agricultural curriculum seemed to anticipate future criticisms that such agricultural/industrial courses were class biased, fixing the status of the children of the poor: "Students here are not pauperized, nor do they suffer from paternalism."[40]

Uncertainty exists about how much Principal Stoltzfus believed in the agricultural curriculum. Under her administration, it was reorganized into three four year courses: Latin, English-science, Agricultural-industrial. Her private correspondence reveals an enthusiasm for the humanities:

> I wish you could see how these young people have improved. When we began the majority of the young men had little ambition beyond riding fast horses and carrying fire arms. They refused to study English and History, but by use of tact they have become very much interested in both subjects. The boys debating club, which meets once a week, now prefers historical subjects.[41]

There was sometimes a note both of defensiveness and of reassurance about the agricultural curriculum. Parents were assured that "the modifications were not so great" that graduates would not be accepted to colleges.[42] Indeed, much of the "Agricultural Course of Study" *was* general education, including "four years of English, four years of Mathematics, four years of Science . . . and two years of either History or German."[43] In case this curriculum seemed more college prep than agricultural, the catalog announced that all subjects could be given a "countrylife twist" and it was the aim of the school to have all subjects "surrounded by an agricultural halo."[44]

The issue about which there is little ambiguity is gender bias. Different sex roles were clearly defined and were reflected in different aims and curricula. In documents related to the school, different roles for women were treated as matters-of-fact and were non-controversial. Such attitudes are to be expected of turn of the century America, especially in the South, but, nevertheless, it is instructive to see that they were played out in a particular time and place.

The stated aims of Farragut made the different sex roles explicit: "To make better and wiser husbandmen of the country boys, and more economical and skillful housewives of the farmers' daughters."[45] The agricultural course for women was justified on the basis of life adjustment: "Practically all of them become farmer's wives." True, some might use their agricultural knowledge as country school teachers, but the typical graduate would find her life work and fulfillment as her farmer husband's helpmate and as mother to his children. Agricultural training was especially valuable for rural mothers, for it provided the "inspiration and stimulus for agricultural pursuits given to boys and girls to the next generation by educated mothers who understand the principles of agriculture and who have real sympathy for country life."[46] Some catalogs end similar quotes with "mothers who are in sympathy and love with country life."[47]

Gender differences were reflected in daily school activities. After commenting on the boys' work with crops, vineyards, orchards, and cattle, Chesnutt, the agriculture teacher, reported that the girls were engaged in "flower culture": "The hill has not been without lots of flowers since the crocus bloomed in April."[48] But, of course, some homemaking skills were more important than growing flowers. In the second year sewing class, as an example, women students learned "the use of the needle, the highest of the feminine arts."[49] Some of the courses such as Household Economics, which was to "help relieve the awful drudgery of women's work on the farm," were more explicitly related to what were considered women's jobs such as dairying. Female students were taught "scientific methods of butter-making and caring for milk for use on the table and in the sick room. . . . "[50] However, women at Farragut, as public school students everywhere, needed most of all to be instilled with the proper values. An aim of the school was "therefore to train girls to work intelligently, to be neat, systematic and quick and above all to be happy in performing the daily duties of a home."[51]

Conclusion

A historical case study is significant for what it illustrates and exemplifies as well as for the pesky anomalies it reveals. Some southern communities might exemplify the themes of this book in a less ambiguous way. Still, there is much in the historical data on Farragut School that supports revisionists' treatment of the southern progressives and critical historiography generally. Most of the people in the community may have supported the establishment of a high school, but the form of the school was likely imposed by professional outsiders without and a small clique of the wealthy within the community. Farm families may or may not have had a well-developed conception of the school that they wanted, but they were no match for Claxton and his colleagues who were armed with a well-articulated vision of quality education, "scientific" evidence, and the promise of Yankee dollars.

If attempts at social control include efforts by higher social classes to deliberately and systematically impose values

on those beneath them (to "teach the ignorant a better
way"), evidence that social control was a conscious aim of
the school is conclusive. Certainly values related to proper
sex roles were integral. Gender bias was pervasive, but it
was more a reflection of the conventional wisdom of turn of
the century America than anything unique about southern
progressives or Farragut School—an explanation, but not a
justification. And agricultural education may have been
class biased in that it prescribed a proper role for the sons
and daughters of farm families. But, more significantly, it
prepared most of the youth of the community for a nonexist-
ent future. The southern progressives often had a streak of
reaction. They were agrarian romantics who wished to recreate an idyllic, if imaginary, rural society. They did not
foresee the effects of technology, industrialization, and ur-
banization on rural America. Most of the graduates of Farragut, even in its first decade, became urban dwellers, not
farmers.[52]

In the introduction to this book, Kincheloe and Pinar
analyze the critical notion of human agency. Among other
things, this concept includes the idea that persons can influence the forces acting on them; they can take what they
want from what others are trying to impose and resist the
objectionable. The farm families found much to their liking
in Farragut School. They seemed to welcome the school as a
community center. The library, athletic facilities, and, especially, the baths were well used and highly appreciated. Isolation was reduced by the social life centering on the school.
The agricultural curriculum may have been appreciated by
some, but it did not have to be taken too seriously by those
who had visions of an alternative future. Funding agencies
and agrarian romantics got an agricultural school; upward
and outward mobile families got a comprehensive high
school. Such are the compromises that form the American
public school curriculum.

2

Organized Prayer and Secular Humanism in Mobile, Alabama's, Public Schools

Joseph W. Newman

Down in Mobile they're all crazy, because the Gulf Coast is the kingdom of monkeys, the land of clowns, ghosts and musicians, and Mobile is sweet lunacy's county seat. I can tell you that's the truth. I know.

Eugene Walter, The Untidy Pilgrim

South of the salt line is another world. It's more southern than anyplace you've ever lived or visited, more South than Deep South. It's where the fiery Mediterranean temperament— the French and Spanish—clashes with the cooler Anglo attitude which migrated down from the Bible Belt. It's where the Black struggles to maintain his rich African culture.

Tom Perez, " Leopold Explains 'The Salt Line' "

When Ishmael Jaffree went to court in 1982 to stop organized prayer in the Mobile County Public Schools, his suit became a link in a chain of precedent setting litigation. First the *Mobile v. Bolden* voting rights case (1980), then the *Wallace v. Jaffree* school prayer case (1985), then the *Smith v. Board of School Comm'rs* case (1987)—three suits that originated in one city during a single decade took on national significance as they moved through the federal courts, shaping education and politics across the Unites States. Why Mobile? Why did all these cases begin in an Alabama seaport tucked away on the upper Gulf Coast, well outside the national mainstream? The answers are wrapped up in the concept of place.[1]

Mobile as a Special Southern Place

Mobile is one of the South's most remarkable cities. With its roots in a diversity of cultures, Mobile is an unusually heterogeneous pocket of the South. Founded as a fort by the French in 1711, captured by the English in 1763, and the Spanish in 1780, Mobile came into the United States in 1813 as part of the West Florida territory. When Alabama became a state in 1819, Mobile was its largest city by far, a port that would reach the peak of its commercial influence in the 1850s. During the golden age of the cotton kingdom, Mobile was a magnet for people involved in turning cotton into money. Southerners, Northerners, immigrants, merchants, laborer, slaves, Whites, Blacks, Creoles, Protestants, Catholics, Jews—Mobile pulled them in. After the Civil War, many of their descendants stayed on, playing out their respective roles in a community that grew slowly and changed little until World War II.[2]

Now a metropolitan area of 450,000, Mobile maintains a distant relationship with the state of Alabama. More similar to New Orleans or Pensacola than Birmingham of Montgomery, Mobile is a province of the "Kingdom of the Gulf Coast." Were it not for New Orleans, of which Mobile has long been envious, Mobile would be the capital of the kingdom. The first celebration of Mardi Gras in the United States, Mobilians are quick to point out, took place in their city, and only later was the custom exported to New Orleans. Putting such rivalries aside, however, Mobilians admit their affinity with other residents of the Gulf Coast, just as they feel a sense of geographical and cultural separation from people who live farther north.

South of the salt line—the point at which a traveler can first smell the ocean—is indeed a special place. Mobile playwright Tom Perez says the Gulf Coast is "more South than Deep South." The rest of the region, like the rest of the nation, views this place with curious eyes. Where else could Mardi Gras revelry and fundamentalist Christianity exist side by side? Only in a place in which Roman Catholics are present in sufficiently large numbers (about 15 percent of the population in Mobile, well over twice that figure in New Orleans) to constitute an influential minority. French Catholics brought the midwinter carnival with them to the Gulf Coast, where many Protestants quickly joined in the ritual that gives a once a year dispensation to all manner unchurchly goings-on.

Paradoxical behavior? Certainly, but as Joe Kincheloe and William Pinar point out in their introductory essay, Southerners have a high tolerance for paradox. Mardi Gras fundamentalism is simply a south-of-the-salt-line variation on this regional theme, albeit a most peculiar variation to people unfamiliar with the cultural history of the Gulf Coast. Mobile is home to the two largest Southern Baptist churches in Alabama, one of which has sponsored billboards warning: "Christians: Mardi Gras Is Not of God." All but the most fundamental fundamentalists, however, merely smile at the billboards, for the less restrictive Catholic attitude has rubbed off on the city's Protestants. Party on Fat Tuesday, pray on Ash Wednesday.

Prayer is important in Mobile—especially *symbolic* prayer. This chapter highlights local actors and local circumstances, but at the outset I must acknowledge the popularity of symbolic prayer throughout the region and the nation. Public opinion polls show that Americans support prayer in public schools by more than a 2 to 1 margin, and among all Americans, Southerners have been most willing to translate their support into defiance of the law. Southern school systems held onto the tradition of organized prayer long after the U.S. Supreme Court decisions in the *Engel v. Vitale*

(1962) and *Abington v. Schempp* (1963) cases. Many people who attended public school in the South during the 1960s recall that the court decisions were a catalyst for prayer. With the rise of the New Right in the late 1970s and the election of Ronald Reagan in 1980, organized prayer was as deeply entrenched as ever in many southern school systems. And so it was in Mobile.[3]

New Right politicians have found especially fertile ground in Mobile. In 1982, Mobilians helped elect Jeremiah Denton, a native son and former prisoner of war in Vietnam, to the U.S. Senate. The Roman Catholic Denton championed a wide range of social and moral issues in Washington, from opposition to teenage pregnancy and abortion to support for tuition tax credits and school prayer. The state's first Republican Senator since Reconstruction, Denton liked to tell his constituents in Mobile that he was taking their way of thinking to the nation's capital.

Denton easily carried his hometown when he ran for a second term in 1986, but he lost the election statewide. Mobilians are still sensitive about the defeat, and their sense of place colors their sense of loss. As many Mobilians explain the 1986 election, an "outsider" from Tuscaloosa, Richard Shelby, defeated a Mobile "insider." In Mobile there is a tendency to downplay the issues—Shelby ran a hard-hitting media campaign that portrayed Denton as hostile to Social Security—and take the defeat personally, as a rejection of the city.

Many Mobilians view the outcome of Ishmael Jaffree's school prayer suit in the much same way. Overlooking the national significance of the case, Mobilians personalize and particularize the rejection of prayer in the courts. As many see it, a popular local tradition was attacked by an outsider, Jaffree; defended by insiders, a conservative Mobile judge and a New Right Alabama governor; and swept aside by federal circuit court judges and those ultimate outsiders, the justices of the U.S. Supreme Court. Never mind the constitutional issues. Mobile had lost again.

"Place under attack," Kincheloe and Pinar call it in their introduction. This concept also helps explain the Bolden voting rights case, in which Black voters—racial and political outsiders—mounted a challenge to Mobile's at-large elections. Even after the Supreme Court unexpectedly sided with the White majority, the U.S. Congress intervened and changed the standard of evidence required to prove discrimination. At-large elections were soon a thing of the past in Mobile. Place under attack also applies to the Smith secular humanism case, but with a surprising twist. Most Mobilians seemed puzzled rather than threatened by secular humanism. Although Smith was the carefully staged sequel to Jaffree, broad support for purging secular humanism never materialized. A group of insiders from the Jaffree litigation suddenly found themselves on the outside as they tried to convince other Mobilians that a nontheistic religion was in forty-four public school textbooks. Mobile's schools were again under attack, to be sure, but this time most citizens saw the attack coming from the most fundamental of the city's fundamentalists.

Setting the Stage For School Prayer

Ishmael Jaffree is an articulate Black lawyer. He is an agnostic with a Muslim name. His wife is a Baha'i. Jaffree leaves people with the impression of a quiet man who pushes himself to be assertive and sometimes ends up being abrasive. Even his law colleagues say that Jaffree's demeanor clashes with the well-mannered, well-bred image that many Mobilians cultivate. In short, Ishmael Jaffree is a perfectly cast Mobile outsider. Wishing to raise his children with open minds on religious matters, he expected the Mobile County Public Schools neither to advance nor to inhibit religion. Yet every day during the 1981–82 school year, Jaffree's son Choike heard his classmates sing the following prayer—we Southerners usually call it a "grace"—under the direction of their teacher:

> God is great, God is good,
> Let us thank him for our food,
> bow our heads we all are fed,
> Give us Lord our daily bread.
> Amen![4]

Since the beginning of the school year, Choike's teacher had known that the child did not wish to participate in prayer or any other religious exercises, and in March 1982 Ishmael Jaffree told her so, face-to-face, at a parent-teacher conference. The activity was unconstitutional, he contended, following up the conference with a letter reiterating his objections. The school principal learned about Jaffree's complaints and consulted the deputy superintendent, who advised that the prayers could proceed on a "strictly voluntary basis."[5] The class continued to sing grace despite a letter of protest from Jaffree to the superintendent of schools.

Jaffree's other school aged children also found regular religious exercises in their classrooms. Jamel's teacher often sang grace with her students, while in Makeba's class the teacher led grace as well as the Lord's Prayer every day. The principals of the schools these children attended were also aware of Jaffree's objections, but the prayers continued. On May 28, 1982, Jaffree took his complaints to federal district court in Mobile.[6]

During the summer, he broadened his suit, for the Alabama legislature had reacted to the Jaffree case with a bill authorizing prayer—indeed, a specific prayer—in the state's public schools. Governor Fob James, who from 1979 through 1983 was the South's best example of a New Right governor, had engineered passage of the bill. A former Republican, James was the only Democratic governor in the nation who refused to endorse Jimmy Carter in 1980; after the election, he was an unabashed supporter of Ronald Reagan. Quite popular in Mobile, James was born in the central part of the state but maintained a residence at Gulf Shores on the Alabama coast, often calling the Mobile area his "adopted home." The prayer bill that James signed into law in July 1982 provided:

> From henceforth, any teacher or professor in any public educational institution within the State of Alabama, recognizing that the Lord God is one, at the beginning of any homeroom or any class, may pray, *may lead willing students in prayer,* or may lead the willing students in the following prayer to God: Almighty God, You alone are our

God. We acknowledge You as the Creator and Supreme
Judge of the world. May Your justice, Your truth, and Your
peace abound this day in the hearts of our countrymen, in
the counsels of our government, *in the sanctity of our
homes* and in the classrooms of our schools *in the name of
our Lord.* Amen.[7]

James' wife Bobbye had helped lobby the bill through the
legislature, and his son, Mobile attorney Fob III, had com-
posed the prayer.[8]

In an interview that I conducted in April 1985, Jaffree
recalled the effect of the governor's involvement on the
school prayer litigation.

> But for Fob James this case would not have received na-
> tional attention; but for Fob James this case would not be
> pending before the Supreme Court now. . . . [He] called a
> special session of the state legislature, . . . and he said that
> he had heard that three teachers had been sued in Mobile
> and that he wanted to support those three brave teach-
> ers. . . . Once he did that and it got broadcast on PBS tele-
> vision across the state, all of a sudden the media got
> interested. . . . He had the audacity to pose legislation that
> included a prayer, which was clearly the same type of case
> that was found unconstitutional in [1962].[9]

James said he hoped someone would challenge the law
to give the Supreme Court a chance to "reverse itself" on
school prayer.[10] He did not have to wait long for the challenge, for Jaffree quickly expanded his suit to include the
James legislation as well as another Alabama school prayer
law, a little known silent meditation statute:

> At the commencement of the first class of each day in all
> grades in all public schools, the teacher in charge of the
> room in which each such class is held may announce that a
> period of silence not to exceed one minute in duration shall
> be observed for meditation or voluntary prayer, and during
> any such period no other activities shall be engaged in.[11]

The federal district court judge who heard the Jaffree case was W. Brevard Hand, a Richard Nixon appointee. Judge Hand is sometimes called "Reversible Hand" (or, less kindly, "Unlearned Hand") because of the high percentage of his decisions that have been overturned on appeal. Hand, a Methodist, was eager to hear a case involving religion and public education. According to Jaffree, the prayer case had been originally assigned to another judge, but Hand maneuvered to bring it into his own courtroom. At a preliminary hearing held in August 1982, Hand heard Governor James' son argue that "this Court has no jurisdiction over the issues because prayer flows from the Almighty and neither this Court nor any court has jurisdiction over the requirements of the Lord or the prayers of his people."[12] Hand dryly responded, "The Lord is not a defendant in this case; the state is."[13] At the conclusion of the hearing, the judge quoted Matt. 6:5, the verse in which Jesus advises his followers to pray secretly in their closets rather than publicly in the manner of hypocrites.[14] Hand issued a preliminary injunction against the enforcement of the two state prayer laws.[15]

If the injunction pleased some people—a brief filed later by the American Civil Liberties Union (ACLU) praised Hand's "flawless" analysis[16]—it upset others. Jaffree learned that a Moral Majority group contacted the judge and urged him to reconsider his position. In September, Governor James took the unusual step of asking the U.S. Supreme Court to deny Hand jurisdiction over the case. After flying to Washington with his wife and son and inviting one hundred reporters to a press conference, James was embarrassed when the clerk of the Supreme Court informed him that bypassing the normal appeals process would be a practical impossibility.[17]

Actually both the supporters and detractors of Judge Hand should have read his injunction more carefully, for it contained ample clues to the decision he would render in the Jaffree case. The injunction also foreshadowed Hand's decision in the Smith secular humanism case. In a footnote the judge stated:

It is common knowledge that miscellaneous doctrines such as evolution, socialism, communism, secularism, humanism, and other concepts are advanced in the public schools. Teachers adhering to such tenents [sic] are more likely to expose their students to these ideas. Reading, teaching or advancing Biblical principles however is strictly prohibited. It is time to recognize that the constitutional definition of religion encompasses more than Christianity and prohibits as well the establishment of a secular religion.[18]

Hand warned in the main text of the injunction that

if the courts are to involve themselves in the proscription of religious activities in the schools, then it appears to this Court that we are going to have to involve ourselves in a whole host of areas, such as censoring, that we have heretofore ignored or overlooked.[19]

Yet another strong clue came in the concluding paragraph of the injunction, in which Hand declared that "the state may not prohibit students or teachers who wish to pray, whether publicly or privately, from doing so except in very limited circumstances."[20] Significantly, the judge applied his injunction only to the state laws, and he observed that "without state involvement, it would usually be appropriate for a teacher or child to pray before school, during class recess, at lunch, after school, and during the ride home in the school bus."[21]

Not satisfied with the wide leeway Hand had left, Governor James told the reporters at his Washington press conference that he would encourage Alabamians to ignore the injunction.[22] The remark sent Jaffree and his attorney back to Hand's courtroom.

We tried to hold [James] in contempt, and we had a video film of his statement. . . . The judge looked at it and said, "Well, he was telling people to disobey my order, but I'm not going to slap him on the wrist for that." So he didn't do anything! . . . It was clear then that Judge Hand wasn't serious about the enforceability of his [injunction].

Fob James stood momentarily in the national spotlight that Ronald Reagan was shining on school prayer. Under pressure from his New Right supporters, the president was beginning to push his "social issues" agenda. Three days after James spoke out against the injunction, Reagan used Rosh Hashana, the Jewish New Year, to lobby for his proposed constitutional amendment permitting "voluntary" school prayer.[23]

Back in Mobile, interest in the Jaffree case ran high as the full hearing drew near. At a rally held in late September at Cottage Hill Baptist Church, the second largest Southern Baptist congregation in Alabama, a center of New Right activity in Mobile, and the source of anti-Mardi Gras billboards, the pastor shared his pulpit with a Presbyterian minister, both of them urging parents and teachers to become defendant intervenors in the suit. An audience of 2,500 to 3,000 heard that an unfavorable decision in the Jaffree case could "prohibit the free exercise of religion." The two ministers showed they had indeed read Hand's injunction. Picking up on the judge's broad definition of religion, they decried the influence of secular humanism and asked for volunteers to screen public school textbooks for evidence of humanism "and other secular religions." The three teachers named in the suit received a standing ovation at the rally, which also included a collection for the "Religious Freedom Defense Fund."[24] This fund would underwrite many of the defendants' expenses in the litigation, making it possible for the defense to bring in several high-powered expert witnesses. At least one other rally was held, and by the time the case went to trial, 624 parents, teachers, and other citizens had signed on as defendant intervenors.

School Prayer on Trial

With the stage set for school prayer by local religious leaders, the governor, and the president, Judge Hand heard the Jaffree case on November 15–18, 1982. The testimony fell into three broad categories: statements from Ishmael

Jaffree and public educators on the facts of the case and their feelings about school prayer; the opinions of a legal scholar on constitutional law and history; and the testimony of a variety of witnesses—from elementary school children to philosophy and theology professors—on morality and religion. Drawing on newspaper accounts and my interview with Jaffree, I will try to capture the flavor of the testimony in each of the three areas.

Jaffree told the court he had once been a street corner preacher. His mother, a devout Baptist, had pressured him to enter the ministry, and his entire upbringing had "conditioned" him to accept religion uncritically. Now he was trying to raise his own children differently, he said, but the state was interfering by promoting religion in the public schools.[25] During our interview, I asked Jaffree to elaborate as if he were explaining his position to another parent or a teacher. As he did so, his outsider's perspective came through clearly.

> In a pluralistic society you should realize that [there are] people with different religious viewpoints and different world viewpoints . . . and that for all of these people their particular belief patterns are very sincerely held and very important to them. If you look at this society in that way, you will understand how people such as myself, who are agnostics and who want their children to grow up as free thinkers, do not want . . . the public school system to subtly coerce them into a certain belief pattern. You will also be able to understand how members of so-called "minority" religions in this county, such as Jews, Muslims, and Buddhists, would not want any educator or public official to use the power and authority of the state to encourage their children to believe that one particular set of religious views are right and by definition all others are wrong.

> Since the public school system has so much influence on children and how they grow up and mature and the state has so much influence in general over society, then the state throws its weight . . . behind any type of orthodoxy, that's a tremendous influence. In a pluralistic society the state shouldn't be taking sides. . . . I simply wanted my

children to be free from the coercive effects of teacher-initiated religious activities in the public schools.

Makeba Jaffree's teacher testified that she considered leading her students in grace and the Lord's Prayer part of her duties as an instructor. Since not every teacher sees her job that way, I asked Jaffree if he makes a distinction between teacher-initiated and student-initiated prayer. Would he object if a teacher simply stepped aside and allowed a student to lead a prayer?

> I don't think the public schools with their captive student audience should be used as a forum for anyone leading organized prayers in the class. The only [exception] I would make is for students on their own initiative at their desks saying a prayer to themselves. Any student who wishes to do that has my—pardon the use of the word—blessing. However, when students as part of a classroom routine stand up in front of a class and lead the class in prayer, you turn organized prayer [into] part of the regular classroom activity of the school. You elevate prayer, which is clearly a religious activity, to a level of something that the state, the school system, prefers—something that is considered good.
>
> [Students from nonreligious families] are at a disadvantage . . . [because they think] this is what we learn in school and this is the activity that the schools do every day. . . . Those children are forced to make a decision: either to sit there and participate, perhaps even against their will or against their parents' will, or leave the class and become visible. . . . I can tell you with respect to children they can be very cruel to one another, and for a child to get up and visibly leave a class or for students in a class to know that a child does not believe in prayer or does not want to participate—that child will be ostracized. I know my children became ostracized.

But Makeba's teacher also testified that the child willingly folded her hands and prayed along with her classmates. One of my university students observed a similar situation during her student teaching. To this future teacher, the child's compliance was evidence that Jaffree was "just making trouble." He had no right to complain about "coercion," she argued, admitting she found it difficult to look beyond the immediate situation to see the larger issues. But Jaffree turned this future teacher's argument around during our interview, suggesting the schools and the society had indeed "conditioned" his daughter religiously—against her parents' will.

> My children have become so inundated with the Christian faith that basically, in spite of the fact that neither of their parents is a Christian, . . . my children have become budding Christians. . . . Part of it came from the public schools; part of it came from the environment—other children in the neighborhood where they live. At home some of my children, when they see me looking, will deliberately pray at the table. I almost hate to admit this, but it's true. Prayer at the table—this is something daddy has stopped me from doing, this is something that other children do, so I'm going to do it as well.

> The problem that I have with this is not that I'm opposed to them praying; I'm opposed to them doing something because they've been programmed to do it before they really understand what's going on. . . . I didn't want them to become conditioned, programmed like I was as a child into a particular point of view. My wife, certainly, as a Baha'i doesn't want them to become Christians. . . . Because I'm an agnostic, I would prefer that they had open minds and simply not adhere to any dogma.

During the trial, the defense called several expert witnesses who appeared in court on behalf of the defendant intervenors. One such witness was Dr. James McClellan, a scholar of constitutional law and history and counsel to the Senate Judiciary Committee's Subcommittee on Separation of Powers. His testimony, which laid the foundation for Hand's decision, may be summarized easily. According to McClellan, the establishment clause of the First Amendment was adopted to prevent the federal government from establishing a national religion. The establishment clause was not intended to prevent the state governments from establishing religions, nor was the Fourteenth Amendment intended to apply the First Amendment and the rest of the Bill of Rights to the states. The U.S. Supreme Court, by applying the First Amendment to the state despite these original intentions, has committed "one of the greatest travesties in American constitutional law."[26] McClellan said he was "baffled" by the court's refusal to change the course it has followed since the *Everson v. Board of Education* case (1947).[27] When Jaffree's attorney asked him why the justices of the Supreme Court had not "seen the light," McClellan shot back, "Maybe they don't want to see it." Applause filled the courtroom.[28]

The reaction of the audience to McClellan was mild compared with the response to the moral and religious testimony, most of which concerned secular humanism. Soon it was obvious what the majority of the audience had come to hear. I asked Jaffree to describe the atmosphere in the courtroom.

> I thought it was a religious revival or something. [School prayer supporters] were always there with their Bibles. . . . They had their children in some cases. They marched children up . . . to have them testify that they were offended by some things in the books. They would meet me in the hallway and offer me a Bible and tell me that they were going to pray for me. They told me that God is looking very closely at this trial and is very concerned about what's going to happen.

> The trial became a circus. . . . The judge allowed in evidence on everything: evolution, homosexuality in the textbooks. . . . Hand could have controlled his court. . . . I think Hand was not prepared for what came in, but I guess he was so entertained by it all that he decided just to let it all in.

Two expert witnesses who drew especially strong reactions were Richard A. Baer, professor of philosophy and religion at Cornell University, and R. J. Rushdoony, a theologian from California. Both argued that secular humanism is a religion that has crowded other religions out of the public schools.[29] Rushdoony was vehement as he denounced the influence of secular humanism in the classroom.

> We have the conflict between the generations. Society has rarely seen adolescence in the manner it now exists. The values of the culture are rejected by the children and rebellion sets in. Previously, adolescents were eager to imitate adults. But we now have rebellion as a result of modern education.[30]

Following Rushdoony to the stand was Delos B. McKown, chair of the philosophy department at Auburn University, who testified for Jaffree. McKown, a former minister and now an avowed secular humanist, argued that secular humanism is not a religion. The Constitution advances secular goals,[31] he continued, but "there is powerful religious pressure to get the instruments of state to do evangelism in the schools."[32] The defense cross examined McKown extensively, probing his opinions on such matters as pornography, communism, and premarital sex. the defense strategy was to generalize McKown's views to secular humanists as a group, then find manifestations of those views in the public schools.[33]

The last witness the defense called did just that. A twelve-year-old middle school student told the court that some of her school lessons had given tacit approval to drinking alcoholic beverages and running away from home. She said she had been asked to play the "lifeboat game," a values clarification technique that forces students to determine which of the boat's passengers will live and which will die. Several defendant intervenors had already testified that they had found abundant evidence of secular humanism in the public school textbooks they had examined.[34]

I asked Jaffree for his views on secular humanism. In particular, I asked him to address the Supreme Court's *Torcaso v. Watkins* decision (1961), for several defense witnesses had called attention to the footnote in the case that refers to Secular Humanism (capital S, capital H) as a religion.[35]

I don't deny that there's a group [of people] who refer to themselves as Secular Humanists and have applied for tax purposes as a religion. . . . The mere fact that there is [such a group] does not mean the religion of Secular Humanism is being advanced in the public schools. There's a difference. . . . I don't know of any group of Secular Humanists that meets and says, "Let's foster our religion in the public schools." If in fact that was happening, I would be opposed to it. But [school prayer advocates] can't point to instances where that has happened, so they pick little arbitrary passages out of books—something that makes reference to sex or to a teenager getting pregnant or to evolution—and say, "Aha! That's proof. You see, the textbooks have secular humanism in them, and that's the religion that's being fostered. . . ." It goes from the sublime to the ridiculous. . . .

. . . .

And yet Hand has informed my attorney that if we filed in court to have him enjoin secular humanism, he would get angry because he would think that we were playing. None of the intervenors, interestingly enough. . . . or parties to the lawsuit have asked Judge Hand to include in his order an injunction against secular humanism in the schools. They're so concerned about it—why not ask the court to enjoin that as well? . . . I contacted one of the leaders of the intervenors and asked him if he wanted to go with me jointly and get an order from the court to get rid of the secular humanism in the schools, and he said he didn't want any part of it! That shows you how serious they are about that.

When Jaffree made this statement during our April 1985 interview, which took place two months before the Supreme Court announced its decision in the Jaffree case, perhaps he was simply underestimating how serious Hand and the intervenors were about ridding the schools of secular humanism. Or was Jaffree suggesting, between the lines, how determined they were to frame the next case with their arguments rather than his?

The Jaffree trial ended after four days of testimony. Given the opinions Hand had expressed in the injunction and similar remarks he had made in the courtroom, the defense was confident. Jaffree was pessimistic. "I'm prepared to lose," he said. "I'm prepared to go with all this baggage to the Eleventh Circuit [Court of Appeals]."[36]

"The United States Supreme Court Has Erred"

On January 14, 1983, two months after the trial, Judge Brevard Hand issued a decision so unusual it made news across the nation. "The United States Supreme Court has erred in its reading of history," he declared. "Because the establishment clause of the First Amendment to the United States Constitution does not prohibit the state from establishing a religion, the prayers offered by the teachers in this case are not unconstitutional." In a sixty-six page opinion that amplified the testimony of James McClellan with a detailed analysis of the circumstances surrounding the adoption of the Bill of Rights and the Fourteenth Amendment, Hand rebuked the judicial branch of government for usurping legislative perogative. Casting himself as a latter-day John the Baptist—"a voice crying in the wilderness"—Hand charged that "the judiciary has, in fact, amended the Constitution to the consternation of the Republic."[37] The decision was a strict constructionist, states' rights interpretation of the Constitution just the kind the Supreme Court has reviewed and rejected in similar cases since the late 1940s. Symbolically, Judge Hand was shaking his fist at the Supreme Court. The symbolism was not lost on Mobilians, who saw an unreconstructed insider daring the Washington outsiders to call his bluff.

Hand relegated the secular humanism controversy that had taken center stage in his courtroom to a final footnote. He wrote that secular humanism is indeed a religion, one so deeply embedded in the public schools that "it becomes a brainwashing effort."[38] To ferret it out would be "a never-ending task."[39] Thus, the judge was content to leave undisturbed in the schools secular humanism, Christianity, and all the other doctrines he had called "religions." But Hand promised in unmistakable terms what he would do if his decision were reversed:

> If this Court is compelled to purge "God is great, God is good, we thank Him for our daily food" from the classroom, then this Court must also purge from classroom those things that serve to teach that salvation is through one's self rather than through a deity.[40]

To Ishmael Jaffree and others who object to religion in the schools, Judge Hand offered this advice: "The Constitution . . . does not protect people from feeling uncomfortable. A member of a religious minority will have to develop a thicker skin if a state establishment offends him. Tender years are no exception."[41] And thus the judge dissolved his injunction against the Alabama prayer laws.[42]

Reactions to the decision came quickly. James J. Kilpatrick, who on earlier occasions had dismissed organized school prayer as empty ritual, expressed admiration for Hand's defense of states' rights: "Let it be said that Judge Hand, if only for an hour, raised a beacon that shed a guiding light."[43] The executive director of the ACLU in Alabama said she was "speechless" at Hand's ruling: "He is trying to overturn twenty years of Constitutional law."[44] The Associated Press quoted the reaction of the Moral Majority's executive director in Alabama—"fantastic"—and reported Fob James' praise for Judge Hand: "That man's got guts."[45]

Predictably, some of the most intense reactions came in Mobile. Dan Alexander, president of the Mobile County Board of School Commissioners and executive director of Save Our Schools (SOS), a division of the national Taxpayers Education Lobby, conducted a press conference in a Mobile middle school only hours after Judge Hand had issued his ruling. While the television cameras rolled, students cheered and applauded as Alexander, a Roman Catholic and an attorney, announced the decision. He asked the students what they usually did before they ate lunch. "Pray," they answered. Alexander told the students they could still pray. Those who did not want to pray could leave, he added. No one left as the students recited, "God is great. God is good. Let us thank him for our food. . . . "[46]

As Kincheloe and Pinar suggest in their introductory essay, the line between the private domain and public domain is hazy to many Southerners: "The familial space, the private, extends far beyond its literal dimensions to engulf what is typically understood as public space." If kids can say grace at the dinner table at home, then they should be able to say grace in the lunchroom at school. Who could object to that? Alexander's press conference symbolized the lack of a clear distinction between the public and private domains, for the atmosphere was equal parts political rally, Sunday worship, and Sunday dinner.

Dan Alexander's ongoing involvement with school prayer is a case study in New Right politics. A controversial figure in Mobile, well-known for his hard line advocacy of teacher competency testing and his frequent clashes with the school board's two Black members, Alexander tried to build a more positive image by identifying himself with school prayer. Already he had traveled to Washington on National Prayer Day to confer with President Reagan and make a speech on the Capitol Mall. Alexander featured the Jaffree case in the SOS newsletter, which circulated throughout the nation with the help of Richard Viguerie's mailing lists.[47] Alexander and Jaffree debated the school prayer issue on several television and radio programs. According to Jaffree, Alexander told him the case would help both of their careers, and while the case was in the news Alexander declared his candidacy for the U.S. House of Representatives. He lost the Democratic nomination, however, to a more moderate politician who, in turn, lost the election to Democrat turned Republican Sonny Callahan—the sponsor of Fob James' prayer bill in the Alabama Senate.

Jaffree apealed Judge Hand's decision to the Eleventh Circuit Court in Atlanta. While the court was considering the appeal, Jaffree asked for an injunction, for his children were facing prayer with a vengeance in their classrooms. He had instructed his children to excuse themselves, but

they came home and told me that they felt uncomfortable
being excused because . . . the other children were talking about them and laughing, snickering when they came
back into the room. They just felt very bad. They wanted to
be accepted by the other children, and they didn't want
to leave the classroom. I was faced with the choice of having them stay in—and that was contrary to my philosophy, contrary to what I thought the Constitution required—or having them leave, which created a great deal
of pain for them.

Surprisingly, the circuit court refused to grant the injunction, whereupon Jaffree turned to U.S. Supreme Court
Justice Lewis Powell for an emergency stay.

On February 2, 1983, Powell reinstated Hand's original
injunction while Powell studied the case further. Dan Alexander then told Mobile's teachers they could continue to
lead prayer since Hand's injunction had applied only to the
state prayer laws, not to teacher-initiated prayer.[48] Alexander showed that he, too, could shake his fist at the highest court in the land. Angered by the situation, Powell
issued another ruling on February 11, flatly stating that
"conducting prayers as part of a school program is unconstitutional." Citing the Engel and Abington decisions, Powell
pointed out that "district court was obligated to follow those
Supreme Court decisions even though it believed them to be
in error."[49]

While the circuit court reviewed the Jaffree litigation
during the winter and spring of 1983, religion in the public
schools was one of the hottest issues in Washington. Congress studied several prayer bills, including Reagan's proposed constitutional amendment, and pondered two bills
sponsored by Jeremiah Denton granting religious groups
"equal access" to the public schools. The Alabama senator
led to the White House a delegation that included Senator
Jesse Helms, a representative of Jerry Falwell, a lawyer for
the Christian Broadcasting Network, and other conservatives, seeking the Justice Department's intervention in the
Jaffree case. Secretary of Education Terrel Bell informed a

Senate Judiciary subcommittee that the absence of school prayer was partly to blame for the problems of public education.[50]

On May 12, 1983, the Eleventh Circuit Court of Appeals reversed Judge Hand's decision, citing numerous precedents and stating that the litigation had raised no new issues. A three-member panel unanimously declared both state-sanctioned prayer and teacher-initiated prayer unconstitutional, ordering Hand to enjoin both forms. With George Wallace back in the governor's chair in Alabama—Fob James did not seek a second term—*Jaffree v. James* had become *Jaffree v. Wallace*.[51] Although Wallace and James have little in common, politically or otherwise, Wallace saw the political advantage of asking the circuit court for a rehearing en banc (by the full court). In August the court denied the petition. Four justices dissented, however, arguing that the court should consider the constitutionality of the "silent meditation" law.[52]

After the circuit court ruling, silent meditation became the focus of attention. Governor Wallace and the Mobile County Board of School Commissioners appealed the entire range of issues involved in the case to the U.S. Supreme Court in November 1983, but the Justice Department intervened in support of the meditation statute only.[53] In April 1984, the Supreme Court upheld the circuit court on every part of the case but silent meditation, agreeing to hear further arguments on that one issue.[54] Attorneys representing all parties appeared before the Supreme Court in December 1984, and for six months the justices weighed the evidence.

The Supreme Court Decision

The headlines of the June 5, 1985 *Mobile Register* told the story: "Prayer Advocates Blast Court."[55] On June 4, the U.S. Supreme Court had found Alabama's silent meditation law unconstitutional. In a 6–3 decision, the court had ruled that "the statute was enacted to convey a message of State endorsement and promotion of prayer."[56] Examining the history of the law in more depth than the lower courts, the Supreme Court noted that the original version of the law, passed in 1978, had set aside a one minute period "for meditation." In 1981, the legislature had changed the law to read "for meditation or voluntary prayer." The sponsor of the legislation in the Alabama senate freely admitted that the change was an "effort to return voluntary prayer" to the public schools.[57]

The majority opinion written by Justice John Paul Stevens and the concurring opinions of Justices Lewis Powell and Sandra Day O'Connor suggested that some of the silent meditation laws in twenty-four other states may be constitutional if they do not promote religion so blatantly. As O'Connor wrote:

> The crucial question is whether the State has conveyed or attempted to convey the message that children should use the moment of silence for prayer. This question cannot be answered in the abstract, but instead requires courts to examine the history, language, and administration of a particular statute to determine whether it operates as an endorsement of religion.[58]

Justice Stevens' opinion briefly reviewed the history of the First Amendment as it applies to the states, quoting the Supreme Court's decision in an earlier case:

> If there is any fixed star in our constitutional constellation, it is that no official, high or petty, can prescribe what shall be orthodox in politics, nationalism, religion, or other matters of opinion or force citizens to confess by word or act their faith therein.[59]

"The State of Alabama, no less than the Congress of the United States, must respect that basic truth," Stevens concluded.[60]

The three dissenting justices critiqued the notion of government neutrality with respect to religion. Justices Warren Burger and Byron White asserted that the mere mention of "voluntary prayer" in the Alabama law did not constitute an endorsement of religion, with Burger continuing that the concept of "benevolent neutrality" should allow the state to "accommodate religious needs" in a "noncoercive manner."[61] Justice William Rehnquist presented yet another historical review. Apparently accepting the idea that the Fourteenth Amendment incorporates the First Amendment and the rest of the Bill of Rights, he still insisted that "nothing in the Establishment Clause requires government to be strictly neutral between religion and irreligion."[62]

Given the reactions to the lower court decisions in the Jaffree litigation, the reactions to the Supreme Court ruling were predictable; they seemed almost rehearsed. Dan Alexander, no longer school board president but still head of Save Our Schools, anticipated the day when the minority opinions in the case would be in the majority. "We have to look forward to a changing court in the next four or five years," he said. There was no immediate comment from Fob James, but Governor Wallace echoed Judge Hand's position: "The Supreme Court is in error."[63] James Kilpatrick lost little time in terming the decision "pure absurdity."[64]

The ruling disappointed Ronald Reagan and Jeremiah Denton, but it came at a politically opportune time for the Alabama senator. Two days after the decision, Reagan spoke at a Denton fund raising luncheon in Alabama. Calling Denton "my kind of senator," the president turned his attention to school prayer.

> I know that there has been a strong push . . . to help restore voluntary prayer in public schools. As this week's Supreme Court decision shows, we still have an uphill battle before us. So I hope we can also count on the support of Alabama's entire congressional delegation for our prayer amendment, because it is time it was adopted.

Denton's fund raiser took in $600,000, apparently setting a state record.[65]

Ishmael Jaffree expressed surprise and relief at the decision. Legally the ruling was a complete victory. Although the case strained his marriage and upset his entire family Jaffree said he felt vindicated. Not opposed to silent meditation per se, Jaffree nevertheless voiced concern that meditation *laws* might encourage teachers and students to go further. With his attention fixed on organized prayer, Jaffree did not raise the possibility that Judge Hand might reopen the litigation to focus national attention on secular humanism.[66]

A Footnote Becomes a Sequel: The Smith Secular Humanism Case

Hand, however, kept his promise. Three months after the Supreme Court announced its decision, he realigned the parties in the Jaffree case, making the original 624 defendant intervenors (headed by teacher Douglas Smith) the new plaintiffs. The Mobile County Board of School Commissioners, the Alabama State Board of Education, and Governor George Wallace became the new defendants. Hand allowed twelve Mobile County parents to join the litigation as defendant intervenors. Ishmael Jaffree, wearied by the three-year legal ordeal he had just endured, bowed out of the case. He would come to regret this decision, however, for when he later tried to reenter the case, Judge Hand denied his request.[67]

Once again the stage was set for a courtroom battle over religion in the Mobile County Public Schools. As the nation watched, a fascinating cast of characters assembled. With the support of Pat Robertson's National Legal Foundation, lawyers for the fundamentalist plaintiffs prepared to elaborate on the secular humanism arguments that the presiding judge himself had outlined in the Jaffree case. People for the American Way and the American Civil Liberties Union offered legal assistance to all the defendants, but only the twelve defendant intervenors accepted. For a while, in fact, it seemed that the intervenors were the only defendants willing to fight the case in court. The Mobile County Board of School Commissioners and Governor Wallace signed a consent decree admitting that secular humanism is a religion, one that is advanced in the schools to the virtual exclusion of Christianity and Judaism. The Alabama State Board of Education appeared to be on the verge of signing a consent decree, but finally the board decided—by a one vote margin—to stay in the litigation.[68]

During a twelve-day trial that stretched over much of October 1986, Judge Hand's courtroom once again became a forum of opinion on secular humanism. This time the focus was on public school textbooks. The array of expert witnesses was broader and more impressive than before, with well-known conservative Russell Kirk joining philosopher-theologian Richard Baer, philosopher-psychologist William Coulson, and a host of others in support of the plaintiffs. Testifying for the defense were Paul Kurtz, author of the second *Humanist Manifesto,* philosopher Delos McKown, psychologist Robert Coles (who submitted a written brief), and many other witnesses.[69] The deponents for both sides had fine credentials, to be sure, but the atmosphere was different at this hearing. Hand had no trouble maintaining decorum. In fact, he had to order "numbing cold courtroom temperatures . . . to keep observers awake." It struck some observers that the judge, lawyers, and witnesses were just going through the motions. As a reporter for the *Mobile Press-Register* put it, "the nation watches a case many say has already been decided and which others are labeling their Christian call to arms."[70]

Actually, both views of the Smith case were accurate. The plaintiffs, many of them members of Cottage Hill Baptist Church, did indeed see the case as a call to arms. As for the decision, few people who had followed the litigation were surprised when Judge Hand ruled in favor of the plaintiffs on March 4, 1987. Hand chose Ash Wednesday, the day after Mardi Gras, to announce his judgment. Expanding the final footnote in his Jaffree decision into a 172 page opinion, Hand ruled that, for purposes of the First Amendment, secular humanism is indeed a religion; that secular humanism is present in forty-four books on the Alabama State

Approved Textbook List; and that the use of the books in
the public schools is an unconstitutional establishment of
religion. Hand ordered the textbooks removed from the
schools.[71]

It also came as no surprise that on August 26, 1987, the
Eleventh Circuit Court of Appeals unanimously overturned
the decision. The court found that while certain passages in
the textbooks are consistent with the set of beliefs that the
plaintiffs labeled secular humanism, other passages in the
books are consistent with Christianity, Judaism, and other
traditional religions. "Mere consistency with religious te-
nets," the court wrote, "is insufficient to constitute unconstitutional advancement of religion." The overall "message"
that the textbooks convey is neither the endorsement nor rejection of religion; instead, the books represent "a govern-
mental attempt to instill . . . such values as independent
thought, tolerance of diverse views, self-respect, maturity,
self-reliance and logical decision-making."[72] The plaintiffs
were pleased, however, that the court of appeals declined to
rule that secular humanism is not a religion, leaving open
the larger question of what constitutes a religion for First
Amendment purposes.[73]

What *was* unexpected about the Smith case was that
the plaintiffs' call to arms had so little appeal, even in Mobile. The avowedly conservative *Mobile Press-Register* covered the Jaffree case with an obvious bias in favor of
organized prayer. (True to form, the newspaper would brand
as "judicial folly" the Supreme Court's 1989 refusal to review
a lower court prohibition of organized prayer at public school
athletic events.)[74] Yet the *Press-Register* tilted against the
Smith plaintiffs from the moment the case began. In contrast to the June 1985 headlines proclaiming that prayer advocates had "blasted" the Supreme Court's Jaffree decision,
the *Register* announced the circuit court's Smith decision
with "Court Reverses Ban on Textbooks."[75] In contrast to ed-
itorials defending the tradition of school prayer, the *Press-
Register* now argued "Textbook Case Undeserving of Court
Time."[76] The editorialist contended that although textbooks
understate the role of traditional religion in American life:

to accept the fundamentalist plaintiffs' arguments in this case requires a uniquely conspiratorial view of how the world works. They charge a conspiracy of secular humanists. No such conspiracy exists. . . .

. . . .

[A fundamentalist victory would] relinquish authority to set education policy to a small group which seeks to censor textbooks and insert its own sectarian beliefs through a federal judge's orders.

That must not be allowed to happen.[77]

As the "postscript" to this chapter indicates, few Mobilians understood the complex issues that swirled in Judge Hand's courtroom. Few people—public school teachers included—paid attention to the historical arguments over the First Amendent and the philosophical debates over theistic versus nontheistic religions. Several witnesses for the plaintiffs, for example, defined the *presense* of secular humanism as the *absense* of traditional religion. As evidence that social studies textbooks promote the nontheistic religion of secular humanism, these witnesses cited the insufficient number (in their judgment) of references to Christianity, Judaism, and other theistic religions. A major problem with such arguments, as lawyers for both sides discovered in the courtroom, is that they are too abstract to play to the galleries. Trying to prove that something exists by documenting the absence of something else is a theoretical exercise. Regardless of the side one takes, taking part in such a discussion demands critical thinking.

Judge Hand and the fundamentalist plaintiffs made a serious miscalculation by expecting a relatively high level of discourse from the general public. Joe Kincheloe and William Pinar suggest in their introduction that fundamentalists have rarely presented their appeal in such an abstract, theoretical way. Instead, religious fundamentalism has reinforced the "literal mindedness" of Southerners, their disdain for theory and speculation. During the Jaffree litigation, bumper stickers reading, Kids Need to Pray were popular in Mobile. Simple message, vivid image. What would have been the equivalent for the Smith case? "Kids Don't Need Secular Humanism?" Such bumper stickers never appeared, of course, for the case against secular humanism cannot be so neatly summarized. By issuing their call to arms in abstract terms, the plaintiffs were stepping—and arguing—out of character. Ironically, they had overestimated their audience.

Mobilians were not prepared to grapple with the complexity of secular humanism, but they could readily grasp the words of the *Press-Register's* editorialist, such words as "conspiracy," "ban," and "censor." Students and teachers were resentful that school officials, acting under court order, were forced to collect social studies and home economic textbooks two-thirds of the way through the school year. The Smith litigation cast Judge Hand and the most fundamental of Mobile's fundamentalists in the unaccustomed role of outsiders.

Even when the plaintiffs' message got through, few Mobilians heeded their call. If the Mobile teachers who have talked with me are at all representative, most of the small number of local educators, who took the trouble to understand the arguments, rejected Judge Hand's conclusions. Members of the Hillcrest Baptist Church, another Southern Baptist congregation in Mobile, joined with the Unitarian Universalist Fellowship to oppose the judge's decision. But most Mobilians, and I suspect most Southerners and most Americans, never even understood the issues, much less accepted the plaintiffs' position. That may explain why the plaintiffs, apparently at the urging of presidential candidate Pat Robertson, declined to appeal the case to the Supreme Court.[78]

Postscript

The place is Wintzell's Oyster House in downtown Mobile. The time is early 1987, soon after the announcement of Judge Hand's decision in the Smith case. KQED, the PBS television affiliate in San Francisco, is in Mobile doing research on religious freedom in America. Later in 1987, the videotaped footage will air nationwide as part of "We the People," a series of programs celebrating the bicentennial of the U.S. Constitution. Peter Jennings will serve as narrator, and President Reagan himself will introduce the series. Trying to convey a sense of place, Jennings will use powerful symbols to explain Mobile to his viewers. As the cameras show Mardi Gras floats, a drag queen, open consumption of alcohol, and revelry of all sorts, Jennings will observe that:

> at Mardi Gras in Mobile, there seem to be no rules. Anything goes, and freedom of expression is at its most outrageous. Cottage Hill Baptists in Mobile have publicly opposed Mardi Gras, but others in Mobile take great pride in telling you that it is the original Mardi Gras in America.[79]

And tonight, almost two years after the Supreme Court decision in the Jaffree case, the KQED reporter is asking people at Wintzell's if they approve of school prayer. The Black oyster shucker behind the counter answers, "Yes, there should be prayer in school, for them who don't want to say it don't have to." A White man eating at the oyster bar states, with obvious conviction, that:

> If I wanted to bow my head and pray right here, that's my freedom. If my children want to have a prayer before they start school, they should be able to do it. If the people wants to pray, they can pray. They shouldn't dictate religion—any way, any form.

A Black man playing checkers in front of a nearby business agrees. "I think a person should be able to worship in school. I do. I mean, a moment of silent prayer—you know, I can't see where that would hurt anybody." In the televised interviews, not one person expresses opposition to school prayer.

When the reporter asks about secular humanism, however, the answers come with less certainty, even though the Smith case has been in the local news for several months.

The customer enjoying oysters at the bar, firm in his opinions on prayer, confesses that he is:

> not sure exactly what you mean by secular humanism—
> whether you're talking about separation of race of separation of sex. I couldn't give you a definition. I truly couldn't.

A young White man shopping at a suburban mall is better informed: "Secular humanism is basically where you make a god of yourself. You're your own god." But a young White waitress captures the reaction of most Mobilians. "Is it like prejudism or something? Is that it? I wouldn't—I don't know. I mean, it can't be in my school, because I don't know. . . . Is this a trick question?"

Part II

Gender Elements

3

Particularities of 'Otherness': Autobiography, Maya Angelou, and Me

———————— *Susan Huddleston Edgerton*

When I reached teen age in the small town of Ruston, Louisiana, the adult gaze upon me seemed suddenly to reflect a new attitude. Clearly, I was now perceived through different eyes than those who had hitherto seen only the child in me. As a teenage girl I was no longer to be trusted; in particular my moral character was suspected—a bewildering development for one who had exerted so much effort to create and maintain an identity of "good girl." Like Jenny Fields in John Irving's *The World According to Garp,* I was a "sexual suspect." Constantly I was admonished to not to do this or that, else I would "ruin my life." The list of "thou shall nots" was long and detailed. After a few years I came to wonder: What does one do *after* one ruins one's life? At the time, I failed to appreciate fully the insights that question would yield. Now that I have temporal distance from the question, I can better appreciate its capacity to provoke skepticism. It is an autobiographical question that can begin an investigation of what is, including the status quo of race, class, and gender, an investigation particularized in place and person.

Autobiography and Critical Literacy

Autobiographical writing enables students to study themselves. Such study links self to place, and place is simultaneously historical, cultural, and racial. The autobiography of the "other"—indeed an "other" who shares a geographical place can provide, in a sense, a foil to one's own life history. Via another's life one understands more fully one's own, as well as the social and historical ties that link both lives to a particular place, in this instance, the South.

I would argue that the concept of the "other" is crucial to understanding the concept of "place." Place is linked with the construction of "difference," of "them and us," often resulting in exclusion of the "other." The challenge to teachers and other curriculum workers is to teach in ways that reincorporate the excluded and construct a more complex sense of place, one based on "difference." One can experience the comfort of one's place without banishing the "other" through the elimination of difference. As Biddy Martin and Chandra Mohanty observe:

> "Being home" refers to the place where one lives within familiar, safe, protected boundaries; "not being home" is a matter of realizing that home was an illusion of coherence and safety based on the exclusion of specific histories of oppression and resistance, the repression of differences even within oneself . . . Illusions of home are always undercut by the discovery of the hidden demographics of particular places, as demography also carries the weight of histories of struggle.[1]

Understanding "place" in this way suggests the process known as "making the familiar strange" (Greene 1973). The unfamiliarity of the other that has been made manageable via stereotyping can be made strange again, but not in a way that presumes discomfort. Now the "other" is made strange in the exhilaration that derives from exposing "dangerous remembrances" about past experiences that are contrary to the "Word." Such experiences contribute to present understanding, often in unexpected ways.[2]

"Making the familiar strange" also means, in this context, critically examining the cliches by which one has learned to live—cliches expressed not only through language but also via routines, habits, and modes of perception as well. What is their origin? What purposes have/do they serve(d)? What occurs when they are challenged? Are cliches and stereotypes analogous orders of (non) thinking?

Autobiographical writing and literature, which "make the familiar strange," can function as aspects of a process of critical literacy as depicted by Paulo Freire and Henry Giroux.[3] Autobiographical work can function to enable teachers and students alike to "reclaim the authorship of their lives"[4] from those industries and institutions that have dominated the cultural "air waves." Literacy that incorporates and goes beyond technical skill in reading and writing becomes:

> . . . both a narrative for agency as well as a referent for critique. As a narrative for agency, literacy becomes synonymous with an attempt to rescue history, experience, and vision from conventional discourse and dominant social relations.[5]

The rescue of history, experience, and vision can occur through the stories of individuals—individual students and teachers whose experience has been historically under-represented in conventional readings and texts. Critical literacy can be taught in the classroom when space is cleared for students voices—space in which students' own particular histories and forms of knowledge are recognized and respected (Pinar 1988, 270 ff.). Such respect does not romanticize voices or stories; it includes a "referent for critique." As Giroux understands:

> It is important to construct a pedagogy of voice and difference around the recognition that some practices (voices/stories) define themselves through the suppression of other voices, [and] support forms of human suffering . . .[6]

Autobiographical literature and writing can be taught in ways that express those voices and stories suppressed in the southern place. More broadly, such literature and writing can function to lay bare suppression or closure; as such, they serve as a means to explain, illustrate, and underline abstract concepts that illuminate wider social, cultural, and historical dynamics. From the particular the teacher can work to the abstract, and back again to the particular, this time a particular opened up by the abstract, its suppressions, closures, and exclusions exposed.

Maya Angelou

Maya Angelou's autobiographical works provide an exciting opportunity to gain the "lived distance necessary for critical social and self reflection. They are, perhaps, especially appropriate for teachers and students from the deep South. For instance, while Angelou's life was vastly different from my own, our circumstances share certain connective tissues of gender and region. These tissues—once linked to Angelou—function to draw me away from myself, my place, and into my experience of her. Such distancing makes possible the surfacing of excluded material.

I suppose those who warned me not to "ruin" my life would say that Angelou ruined hers, indeed, many times over. While both Angelou and I spent significant segments of our childhoods in the deep South, Angelou was poor and black. Further, she lived during a time when racial prejudice and segregation were more oppressive than during my childhood in the 1950s and 1960s.

Maya Angelou was born on April 14, 1928 in St. Louis. She spent important years of her childhood (ages 3–13) in Stamps, a small town in the southwest corner of Arkansas. She was graduated from high school in San Francisco; then she studied dance and drama in both California and New York. Otherwise, she received no formal education. She has written plays, five autobiographical works, several volumes of poetry, and worked as a singer, dancer, actress and a civil rights activist (Reynolds 1988; Evans 1984, 37).

I heard Angelou speak to the congregation at her former church and to her childhood best friend in Stamps on a PBS program hosted by Bill Moyers. Even mediated by the television screen, the interview was moving. By that time, I had read her autobiographies; her image and voice matched despite the two different media. When Angelou spoke (and the PBS program was no exception), the sounds were poetic and powerful. Her voice was deep with the wisdom born of oppression and risk-taking and struggle, and at the same time it possessed hope and *joie de vivre*. Angelou was raped when she was eight-years old. As an unmarried teenager she bore a son and later she worked as a madam, a prostitute, and a dancer in a strip joint—clearly a life "ruined" by the standards of my southern community. I heard no fear in the voice of one returning to her own southern community that night. There, was however, anger.

Stamps is typical of small, southern towns. It is similar to my own hometown of Ruston, Louisiana. Black and White areas of town are so sharply demarcated that they seemed to be drawn with a chalk marker. To step across one's racial line is to step into a distinctly different culture. It feels dramatic enough to remind one of wading into the sea. For Angelou, even after having been away from Stamps for several years and returning as a celebrity of sorts, reported discomfort stepping over that line. Reluctantly, she returned to Stamps in 1981 to be interviewed by Bill Moyers.

An "outsider" like Maya Angelou understands the White South more completely than do those white Southerners who have never left the region. As Rita Mae Brown observes: " . . . to fall into any minority group means you must learn to understand the majority in order to survive. A minority person knows much more about a majority person than vice versa" (Brown 1987, 39). "Outsiders" are more often faced with overt, externally visible contradictions in their daily experience than are "insiders" whose contradictions have been "resolved" via repression. For instance, many white Southerners experience no contradiction between their professed religious beliefs and racial prejudice. To the outsider, the contradiction is obvious. The recognition of such contradictions constitute a "hidden passage" for the oppressed (Bullock 1967,1).

Contradiction, Double Vision,
and the "Hidden Passage"

In "The Meaning of Dialectics," Bertell Ollman describes contradiction as "the incompatible development of different elements within the same relation, that is to say between elements that are dependent on one another" (Ollman 1986). An instance of Ollman's concept of contradiction and of Bullock's concept of "hidden passage" is the slave system in the U.S. Slaves had to be educated to varying degrees in order to be useful as workers, in particular to satisfy those companionship needs to the master class. However, education provided slaves the possibility of power as their education provided the tools by which to understand the injustice of the system. The status of the White master class became denaturalized as the system's contradictions became visible (Bullock 1967, 1–15).

Dialectical thinkers attribute primary cause to those inner contradictions that comprise a system (Ollman 1986). Change is provoked in order to relieve the tensions that accompany these inner contradictions. Change is thus not always or primarily, as in the commonsensical southern view, due to "outside agitators." In this vein, Georg Hegel postulates a built-in contradiction in the master/slave relationship. According to Hegel the slave becomes more competent and powerful as s/he works, and the master becomes more dependent (Harding 1986, 26). This fundamental dynamic is highly suggestive not only for understanding the dynamics of the slave/master struggle, but also of other struggles as well, including civil rights, feminist, and schoolchildren's rights.

Sandra Harding understands well this idea's pertinence for the feminist struggle. She argues that the feminist standpoint originates in the idea that "men's dominating position in social life results in partial and perverse understandings, whereas women's subjugated position provides the possibility of more complete and less perverse understandings" (Harding 1986, 26). More broadly, the dominant are not provoked by lived contradictions to question a system that seems to so directly benefit them. The dominated, on the other hand, have every reason to question and to search for another order of things. As Freire asks: "Who are better than the oppressed to understand the terrible significance of an oppressive society? Who suffer the effects of oppression more than the oppressed? Who can better understand the necessity of liberation?"(Freire 1970, 29)

In the sphere of the school these dynamics are visible. Consider the example of the so-called class clown. Feeling constrained by classroom rules, these students often appear eager to discover the inner contradictions of the school system. Like any comic, the class clown can be said to have one foot in each culture, that is, the culture of the formal school system and that culture lived "underneath" and "around" the formal system. Like Willis' "lads," class clowns come to understand hidden assumptions of classroom codes as well as the "lived worlds" of their peers, expressing humorously the tensions and contradictions generated (McLaren 1985).

As an adolescent determined to ruin her life, I discovered daily contradictions both inside and outside the formal school system. The cult of the southern "lady," assumptions about White supremacy, the psychosocial regressiveness of fundamentalist Christianity all became visible. I kept asking, "Why do people believe what others have simply 'made up,' especially when what they believe injures others?" A southern girl at that time did not ask such a question. Its asking guaranteed that I enjoyed the opportunity to view the mainstream culture from the outside, as someone "ruined." Of course, there was and is much still to learn about my racial and social conditioning. This conditioning and privilege produced a blindness which, in the past, allowed me to reconcile my social awareness with material comforts gained historically from the very contradictions I held in disdain. However, being ruined provides a passage from the culture of that conditioning to another one glimpsed, one to be constructed from the ruins of the old one.

Alice Walker speaks of the importance of a "double vision" for the socially conscious southern black writer. She observes: "For not only is he in a position to see his own world, and its close community, but also he is capable of knowing, with remarkably silent accuracy, the people who make up the larger world that surrounds and suppresses his own" (Walker 1983, 19). Not generally considered a southern writer, James Baldwin expresses a similar view:

> ... the doctrine of White supremacy which still controls most White people, is itself a stupendous delusion: but to be born black is an immediate, a mortal challenge. People who cling to their delusions find it difficult, if not impossible to learn anything worth learning: a people under the necessity of creating themselves must examine everything, and soak up learning the way the roots of a tree soak up water.[7]

Indeed, the oppressor must discover and recreate his or her humanity.

As the southern black experience informs the entire southern White experience, then the experience of southern black women contributes yet another dimension to understanding the southern place. The southern black woman faces a double challenge: not only must she fight for her humanity in a sea of White oppression but she also fights for it as well among blacks. Maya Angelou understands:

> The Black female is assaulted in her tender years by all those common forces of nature at the same time that she is caught in the tripartitie crossfire of masculine prejudice, White illogical hate and Black lack of power.

> The fact the adult American Negro female emerges a formidable character is often met with amazement, distaste and even belligerence. It is seldom accepted as an inevitable outcome of the struggle won by survivors and deserves respect if not enthusiastic acceptance.[8]

Angelou is a formidable woman.

Private/Public Relationality

As noted, contradictions within a system function as catalysts for resistance and change. Analogously, contradictions within the individual person and in their social relations can provoke individual change, change that is essential to macro-social change. I do not intend to suggest a simple cause-effect chain. Rather, individual and social change are relational; neither can be examined in isolation from the other.

Just as an individual's neurosis can be understood as unresolved contradictions that undermine one's own interests and objectives, social oppression and pain can be viewed as social neurosis. Here neurosis is conceived as unresolved contradictions, maintained by delusion. If the origin of suffering is not located, understood and articulated, then the neurosis remains. School curriculum can be understood in this sense as a form of social psychoanalysis in which learning functions to free blocked material, both individual and social, for the sake of social restructuring. In both individual and in social psychoanalysis, confession is central. When curriculum is understood as social psychoanalysis, autobiography becomes a central educational method.

Individual neurosis can be linked with what has been termed social neurosis (Kincheloe 1988). As Russell Jacoby has shown (1975), the individual ego is a social construction. To work on the individual's life history is to work on a social history. The lived foundations of social change can be built. The intimacy between private and public terrains suggests that curriculum be informed by individual life history, both in materials and in exercises. Reading others' autobiographies (especially those who are viewed as "Other") and writing one's own can lead to the identification of inner contradictions—both in private and public spheres—and serve as "hidden passages" from the status quo to a more just order. Discovery of inner contradictions is key, however.

This work of discovery invokes what has been called "dangerous memory" (Marcuse 1964, 98). It is said to be dangerous to both knower and society insofar as it produces a sense of unrest, a sense of the arbitrary nature of social life and power relations. What *is* becomes visible as socially constructed, not "natural" or what must be. Contradictions that constitute the present cannot be fully grasped unless their genesis is investigated. This investigative process of discovery is, for the individual, psychoanalytic, and for society, historiographical. "Dangerous memories" in both private and public spheres can be discovered and articulated. Just as the transference relationship with the analyst elicits repressed memory in the client, the historian brackets taken-for-granted, searching for contradictions, fissures, and leaks.

The Topography of Autobiography

Autobiographical work can be instructive in this quest for contradictions in both individual and social spheres. Angelou's writing reveals not only her own inner conflicts but also their social origins and concomitants as well. The reader is provoked to a like reflection of herself. So begins a process of reexperiencing the tension, a step prior to healing. Serious autobiography such as Angelou's not only challenges the surface of the individual's self system, in its particularity but it also challenges mainstream concepts of the social system. In so doing, Angelou portrays a vision in which the personal and public are mutually constitutive.

Angelou cites the influence of two extraordinary black women in her coming of age. Her grandmother, Annie Henderson, seemed a model of independence and caring. "Mrs. Henderson not only stalwartly provides for her crippled son and two robust grandchildren, she feeds the Black community during the [Great] Depression and helps keep the White economy from collapse" (O'Neale 1984, 29). Angelou's mother, Vivian Baxter, was even more significant. Angelou writes:

> By no amount of agile exercising of a wishful imagination could my mother have been called lenient. Generous

she was; indulgent never. Kind, yes; permissive, never. In
her world, people accepted paddled their own canoes,
pulled their own weight, put their own shoulders to their
own plows and pushed like hell."[9](G.T., p. 7)

And Vivian Baxter's advice to Angelou was:

> Everybody, his brother and his dog, thinks he can
> walk a road in a colored woman's behind. But you remem-
> ber this, now. Your mother raised you. You're full-grown.
> Let them catch like they find it. If you haven't been
> trained at home to their liking tell them to get step-
> ping . . . Stepping, But not on you."[10] (p. 128)

With roles of powerful women before her as a child,
Maya Angelou's faith in her own possibility becomes under-
standable. Interestingly, these perceptions of her mother
and grandmother are made by a young Angelou. In the faces
of these powerful women, the young Angelou could not see
the inevitable vulnerability and uncertainty. With maturity
comes recognition of the complexity of the human character.
The process of recognition began when she witnessed the
strength of these women undermined. She watched help-
lessly as her grandmother was taunted and called "Annie"
deprecatingly by poor White children. Her powerful mother
was helpless to prevent her lover from raping Maya Angelou
in her eighth year.

My own childhood occurred in, relatively speaking, a
more privileged sphere, a White one. Still we experienced
marginalization, as my parents' views regarding race, class,
and religion were outside the mainstream in Ruston, Louisiana in the 1950s. In fact, our family did not go to church, an
act of rebellion in the Bible Belt. My parents were liberals,
and so therefore was I. I recall the year 1964, the year Lyn-
don Johnson's opponent was Barry Goldwater. Desegregation was the big issue in Ruston. I was sure my parents
were right even though not one other soul in my fourth
grade class agreed with us. Speaking up, supported by the
innocent and naive belief that being "right" was enough to

ensure a sympathetic audience, I was assaulted with what seemed to be an interminable chant by the entire class. "Nigger lover! Nigger lover!" they chanted at me. Then "Goldwater! Goldwater!" I felt shock and hurt; the response of my classmates was incomprehensible to me. As I reflect now on my upbringing with the distance time and education can bring, I believe my own liberalism was informed by the same fears as my classmates' bigotry. Rather than convert fear to hatred, my family converted it to liberalism: "They're just like us." Both strategies function to eliminate difference and "otherness."

As a young adult, Angelou lived alternately with or near her mother. Worrying that she lacked traditional feminine beauty, and feeling inadequate due to racism, in this state of vulnerability, she married "because he asked." Her husband was White, although in her eyes his Greek ethnicity made him forgivably White. Displeased with her daughter's engagement, Vivan Baxter moved away three days before the ceremony. Filled with visions of upward mobility. Angelou proceeded.

> We rented a large flat, and on Tosh's orders I quit my job. At least I was a housewife, legally a member of that inevitable tribe of consumers whom security made fat as butter and who under no circumstances considered living by bread alone, because their husbands brought home the bacon. I had a son, a father for him, a husband and a pretty home for us to live in. My life began to resemble a Good Housekeeping advertisement. I cooked well-balanced meals and molded fabulous jello desserts. My floors were dangerous with daily applications of wax and our furniture slick with polish.[11]

Angelou was leading the very life she held in such disdain at age fifteen when she described her stepmother as being a part of the Black bourgeoisie who was "mean and petty and full of pretense" (C.B., 194). The scene provokes images of white picket fences, a Betty Crocker fantasy of a working class, inner city Audrey in "Little Shop of Horrors," or Tracy Chapman's line: "We'll move out of the shelter; buy a big house and live in the suburbs."[12]

Peeling a layer of naïveté, Angelou left that marriage, and worked her way into "show business"—singing, dancing and eventually acting. After a world tour with *Porgy and Bess*, she returned to California, and worked in clubs for a while. Then she and her son Guy moved into a houseboat commune with a few avant-garde Whites. After that episode, she developed an interest in writing. The writer John Killens convinced her to move to New York and join the Harlem Writers Guild. This event marks the political and intellectual awakening of Maya Angelou: "I made the decision to quit show business. Give up the skintight dresses and manicured smiles. The false concern over sentimental lyrics. I would never again work to make people smile inanely and would take on the responsibility of making them think" (Heart 44–45). After hearing Martin Luther King, she and Godfrey Cambridge, feeling that they must participate in the Civil Rights Movement, organized and developed a musical, comedic dramatic revue to play at the Apollo Theater in Harlem, to benefit the Southern Christian Leadership Conference (SCLC). The theme was liberation; the show was a "hit." From this point on Angelou's work was devoted, for the most part, to supporting the civil rights struggle.

To the casual observer, Angelou would appear to be a woman who was as much in control of her life as anyone might be. Her autobiographical accounts reveal a more complex situation. Further, this autobiographical writing functioned to help her resolve some of the conflict and pain in her life. Such a potential of autobiographical work recommends that work, particularly, for the fragmented and alienated. The self that is revealed and constructed by such work can be characterized as, in Sondra O'Neale's term, a "composite self." O'Neale notes:

> "The process of autobiography is not a singular statement of individual egotism but an exultant explorative revelation that she is because her life is an inextricable part of the misunderstood reality of who Black people and Black women truly are."[13] (O'Neale 26).

One aspect of this misunderstood reality is suggested by what constitutes "beauty" in the United States. Traditionally, beauty has functioned to reduce women to the status of sexual object. Furthermore, beauty has not been black. Clearly, African-American women stand to be doubly victimized here. Angelou writes of her feelings about her own appearance. In the following, she describes her feelings as a young child.

> Wouldn't they be surprised when one day I woke out of my black ugly dream, and my real hair, which was long and blond, would take the place of the kinky mass that Momma wouldn't let me straighten? My light-blue eyes were going to hypnotize them, after all the things they said about "my daddy must of been a Chinaman" because my eyes were so small and squinty. Then they would understand why I had never picked up a Southern accent, or spoke the common slang, and why I had to be forced to eat pigs' tails and snouts. Because I was really White and because a cruel fairy stepmother, who was understandably jealous of my beauty, had turned me into a too-big Negro girl with nappy black hair, broad feet and a space between her teeth that would hold a number-two pencil.[14] (C.B., p. 2)

As Angelou recalls her child's fantasy of feminine beauty, I am struck by the fact that as a child my hair was long and blond; my eyes were light blue. Yet I, too, never felt I was pretty enough. What I saw in the mirror was a wide nose on a too-skinny, gate-mouthed face with features so pale as to be invisible—and I behaved accordingly, for the most part, with a level of shyness that insured invisibility. From childhood on we are told we are not quite enough. For those girls who internalize fully the link between self-worth and physical beauty (a physical beauty that can always be improved, and hence is never adequate), powerlessness becomes complete.

As an adult, Angelou persists in referring to herself as one who is "not pretty." This self-concept does not seem to coincide with the facts. From years of dancing her body was strong and healthy. Intellectually she is perceptive, even wise. Yet the culture industry persuaded her that she was inadequate physically.

After the "hit" at the Apollo Theater, Angelou worked for the SCLC, and gained acceptance in the Harlem Writers' Guild. She contemplated a second marriage, this time to a bailbondsman who had little in common with her and who regarded her work at the SCLC as just another job. She describes meeting his family:

> His family treated me with courtesy, but the looks they traded with each other spoke of deep questions and distrust. What did I want with their brother? A grown woman who had been in show business and the Good Lord knows what else. Her teenage son, whose sentences were threaded with big words, who talked radical politics and went on protest marches. What was Tommy going to do with them? And for goodness' sake, she wasn't even pretty, so what did he see in her? If they had asked me, instead of each other, I could have informed them with two words: sex and food[15] (Heart, pp. 100–101).

Plans to marry this man were interrupted only because she met another man who seemed to her to be perfect. The perfect man Angelou found was a South African freedom fighter, who had been a lawyer, was an intellectual, seemed to appreciate her work and talents, and could charm and move a crowd with his speaking ability. The perfection was an illusion. Angelou found herself back in the midst of what sometimes seemed to be irreconcilable conflict. Despite his charm and "political correctness," her lover failed to transport his egalitarian commitments home. He held a gender-based double standard toward domestic labor and sexuality that became, after time, intolerable. Yet to resist his sexism felt like treason to the cause of anti-racism.

Marriage to this man also meant moving to Africa. Angelou expresses her excitement that she would, racially speaking, be returning "home," the site of her ancestral origins, a place where Black people controlled both the public and private spheres. When she went to Africa, she found a different place, one where many residents were disdainful of her nationality just as many White Americans were disdainful of her race. Still she writes of powerful psychological experiences accompanying her travels in places around the continent to which her geneaological studies alerted her. The fact that it was Black people who built and managed the public sphere in Africa helped to exorcise from her vestiges of an internalized inferiority.

Displacement is familiar to me as well. Due to my political commitments and to my way of life, I feel displaced from the southern culture I knew as a child. The displacement becomes significant in that one cannot simply choose another place that is truly home. The place called "home" is in many ways closer to being a part of the anatomy than mere geographic location. But the important difference here is that my displacement holds an element of choice perhaps not available to Angelou. For Angelou, the power of place in Africa derived primarily from the sense that it was home for ancestors who were involuntarily and violently wrenched from the land and sold into slavery, and the displacement that they felt was destined to be passed onto generations of offspring. Thus, there was, for her, a sense of Africa as home that I could never emulate by moving to England, Ireland, or Scotland. As a White person in this situation it is easy to feel a sense of almost envy along with guilt for my privilege that was gained through exclusion and fear of difference. The envy is, in part, *over* this issue of guilt. Minnie Bruce Pratt, in "Identity: Skin Blood Heart" warns:

> In order to feel positively about ourselves, we may end up wanting not to *be* ourselves, and may start pretending to be someone else. Especially this may happen when we start learning about the strong traditions of resistance and affirmation sustained for centuries by the very folks *our* folks were trying to kill.[16]

Angelou and Southern Place

The dynamics of oppression and power relations explicated abstractly in curriculum theory are made concrete in the works of Maya Angelou. She describes hegemony, reproduction, and resistance in ways that make these phenomena accessible to readers unfamiliar with curriculum theory. Further, these abstractions can be seen in the flesh in the context of the deep South, about which many Americans lack full understanding.

Racism leaves Angelou feeling angry with African-Americans' relative acceptance of it, and simultaneously profoundly sympathetic with their plight. She describes the fear that builds from numerous beatings and lynchings, so strong and everyday that the Black woman's "heartstrings [are] tied to a hanging noose. Any break in the routine may herald . . . unbearable news. For this reason, Southern Blacks until the present generation could be counted among America's arch conservatives" (C.B., p. 95). She describes how the Church is complicit with racism: "I find it interesting that the meanest life, the poorest existence, is attributed to God's will, but as human beings become more affluent, as their living standard and style begin to ascend on the material scale God descends the scale of responsibility at a commensurate speed" (C.B. p. 101).

The Church has also functioned as a source of resistance. Martin Luther King, Jr., was brilliant in his use of the Church to support the morality of his civil rights actions. Traditionally, southern Black churches employed more subtle, albeit less publicly effective methods for supporting resistance. Angelou cites one such example when the preacher at her Stamps, Arkansas church began his sermon by quoting from a passage in Corinthians on the necessity of charity. A rousing sermon follows: "Charity don't say, 'Because I give you a job, you got to bend your knee to me.' It don't say, 'because I pays you what you due, you got to call me Master.' It don't ask me to humble myself and belittle myself. That ain't what charity is." The congregation, Angelou reports, "had been refreshed with the hope of revenge and the promise of justice" (C.B., 107).

Angelou expressed her sense of the South as a series of opposites. In the following passage the beauty and sensuality of the natural environment is contrasted with the residue of racism and classism.

In my memory, Stamps is a place of light, shadow, sounds
and entrancing odors. The earth smell was pungent, spiced
with the odor of cattle manure, the yellowish acid of the
ponds and rivers, the deep pots of greens and beans cooking for hours with smoked or cured pork. Flowers added
their heavy aroma. And above all, the atmosphere was
pressed down with the smell of old fears, and hates, and
guilt.[17]

Yet, the South attracts: "Despite the sarcastic remarks of
Northerners . . . ,the South . . . can be so impellingly beautiful that sophisticated creature comforts diminish in importance"(G.T., 64).

Many other artists—both Black and White—have written similarly about the South. The South offers a unique
sense of community that comes, perhaps, from shared poverty, natural disasters, southern violence, as well as from a
shared appreciation of the beauty of the natural environment. The creativity of the southern artist is linked at one
end to the unique characteristics of southern life—both its
nurturing constricting community—and, for those who escape, the other end is linked to a vision of the South provided by vantage points outside the South. This vision is
gained via reading, imagination, even physical exile. For
those who do escape one observes a perhaps unique sense of
dignity. That derives, perhaps, from an experience of the
self that persists and strengthens despite conflict, racism,
stupidity. Southern dignity is built upon rebellion against
provinciality.

What's Place Got to Do with It?

My own sense of the South is of a place where one took
risks in spite of admonitions about ruination and hell. I am
reminded of songwriter Gary P. Nunn's line: "If a Texan fan-
cies he'll take his chances, chances will be taken, that's for
sure."[18] Sometimes verging on compulsion, this courage ex-

acts a price. For me there has been always a sense of something missing. I tried to fill that emptiness with lists of those things to which I looked forward. I complained to my parents that "nothing exciting ever happens here or to us." The emptiness of mindless consumerism contrasted with the fullness of the natural world.

To the southern place I attribute a sense of wonder. The fullness of the natural world meant a sensuality toward the earth. Smells were particularly powerful for me, even figuring into my early career plans when I became a chemist. There is stability in the world I reject, including in the interpersonal world. Twelve to twenty year friendships that began in my adolescence are still alive and well and very much tied to my southern experience. I suppose I still cherish, at times at least, the red-neck girl within me who still has the urge to throw a six-pack of beer in the car, tear down the highway, drinking and screaming with the radio at top volume.

In the attempt to make sense of this in light of what I have learned from Maya Angelou, two related but subtly different terms come to mind, angst and alienation. I think that the distinction between them is important for differentiating Angelou's southern experience from my own. Alienation is estrangement, a sense of lost connection, displacement in the midst of place. Angst is not so much a result of being disconnected as being dissatisfied with the connection. It derives from raised expectations, privilege, the "is that all there is" question. Angst is more of an internalized, private sense derived from social circumstances, but the "angst-ridden" is often unaware of the connection to social circumstances. Alienation is, perhaps, *less* internalized or at least more distanced from one's sense of the natural order. The alienated are, I believe, closer to having a sense of the social construction of alienation-producing circumstances. Clearly, what Angelou experienced was alienation when she wrote: "If growing up is painful for the Southern Black girl, being aware of her displacement is the rust on the razor that threatens the throat. It is an unnecessary insult" (C.B., 3). While some of my negative experience of the

South is tied to alienation—discomfort with Southern sexism, racism, and fundamentalism—my most embedded experiences, as described above, are closer to angst. The common thread between us seems to lie more within our positive experience of the South—nature, smells, risktaking, and music. These are the connections between us that are easiest to explore, and probably, therefore, less important than our differences. These are the connections that introduce us to one another. Our difference functions as a foil, forcing me back onto myself. I came to realize with Minnie Bruce Pratt:

> Then I understood that I was using Black people to weep for me, to express my sorrow at my responsibility, and that of my people, for their oppression: and I was mourning because I felt they had something I didn't, a closeness, a hope, that I and my folks had lost because we had tried to shut other people out of our hearts and lives.

> Finally I understood that I could feel sorrow during their music and yet not confuse their sorrow with mine, or use their resistance for mine. *I needed to do my own work*: express my sorrow and my responsibility myself, in my own words, by my own actions.[19]

Conclusion

The autobiographical method I have explored here involves a critical reading of literature (in the present instance, Maya Angelou's autobiography) that is linked with one's "home" or place. This method utilizes literature and place as occasions to study sameness and otherness, identification and alienation, how our constructions of ourselves are inextricably linked with our constructions of the "other." Place is both figure and ground, source, and destination. It is simultaneously a given and a construction, a beginning point and a mediation. As William Pinar observes:

> Our life-histories are not liabilities to be exorcised but are the very precondition for knowing . . . the situation speaks through the self and the self through the situation. . . . Au-

tobiographical method can be employed to cultivate such attention: to situation as element of the self, the self as situation, and the transformation and reconstitution of both.[20]

Understanding of self is not narcissism; it is a precondition and concomitant condition to the understanding of others (Pinar 150).

While this work is generally useful in gaining more complex and subtle understandings of "self and other" and thus important for all who teach, I see a particular usefulness for teacher education. It is axiomatic that teachers must be well-acquainted and comfortable with themselves if they are to discriminate between and respect both difference and sameness. Clearly, variations of this method may be useful for teachers in a variety of classroom settings, but with the caution that certain dangers inhere. Students can become more vulnerable with autobiographical disclosure. Or students might make superficial revelations, with a glibness that ensures no authentic self-investigation can occur. The teacher who employs autobiographical method must have completed extensive autobiographical work. Further, teachers must tolerate and indeed promote a wide range of variations of method.

Teaching teachers is an order of meta-teaching. We must do that which we attempt to describe. Our teaching method must exemplify our teaching theory. Autobiographical method allows the possibility of such congruence, even when employed to separate oneself from the facticity of one's place.

4

Wrenched From the Earth:
Appalachian Women in Conflict

Kathleen P. Bennett

Introduction

I waited for a response from the twelve graduate students seated in front of me for the initial meeting of a course I was calling "Schooling in Appalachia." My question had been: "How many of you are Appalachian?" To me this was a crucial, straightforward question for the subsequent course work I had planned for these people. Silence. No hands were raised. No response. This was precisely the answer I had anticipated from the students for a variety of reasons—the uncertainty of a first class meeting in which most students did not know me or the other students or, perhaps, the Yankee directness of my question. However, the more probable reason for this silence in response was that I was posing the question to middle-class graduate students from East Tennessee who did not identify themselves as Appalachians. Dwight Billings (1989, 418) reports that "few people in the southern mountains identify themselves as Appalachians."

Stereotypes of Appalachians are overwhelmingly negative. Appalachians are the people portrayed in films like *Deliverance,* comic strips like "Snuffy Smith" and television shows like "The Beverly Hillbillies." Appalachians, derogatorily referred to as hillbillies, ridgerunners, hilljacks, and

briars are portrayed as being lazy, poor, ignorant, dirty, in-
cestuous, clannish, and immoral. Appalachians, particularly
in northern urban areas, are the brunt of ethnic jokes that
affirm and escalate this negative stereotyping. If I had
asked my students if they were Scotch-Irish or southern, the
hands would have been raised. These are acceptable identi-
fiers of cultural and regional backgrounds.

When I had designed this course to be offered as an
elective in the College of Education at the University of Tennessee, Knoxville, my major goal was to have students, who
are primarily teachers, study the history and culture of Appalachian people in order to better understand their own
students in local schools. It would also give me an opportunity to further explore this culture. I had become interested
in Appalachians in the early 1970s when I found myself
teaching in a small rural community in the mountains of
New York state. My classroom was full of Appalachian children whose families had migrated from West Virginia to
work cutting ash trees for use in the manufacture of baseball bats. I later moved to Cincinnati where I worked for ten
years with urban Appalachians in public schools. In my most
recent move to East Tennessee, I feel as though I have returned home to the mountains. Even though I grew up in a
small town on the outskirts of Philadelphia, much of my professional life has been spent either in rural mountain communities or working with families from those areas. I
consider myself at home in these Appalachian mountains.

Since I expected that students who took this course
would be from Appalachian backgrounds, I wanted them to
get beyond the stereotyped notions of Appalachians to the
deeper cultural webs that bind them together as a people.
The best way I knew to do this was through Appalachian
literature. I wanted these teachers to find themselves and
their families in the novels written about the region. By the
end of the course, I wanted them to be able to appreciate
the strength, determination, and independence of Appalachian people.

The purpose of this chapter is to illustrate ways in
which regional literature can be used as primary texts to

develop sociocultural understandings in teacher education. My experiences in the "Schooling in Appalachia" course serves as the basis for this illustration. Throughout the semester, the students and I read Appalachian novels along with our more conventional reading of journal articles about Appalachian culture. The fiction was a powerful way in which to engage students in the lives of Appalachian people, illustrating major cultural themes and conflicts in an emotional as well as intellectual way.

The chapter begins with a discussion of the Appalachian region, providing a geographical and cultural context. Next, I present a discussion of several themes in Appalachian literature that illustrate significant aspects of this culture. In this portion of the chapter, I also explore the lives of Appalachian women—the ways in which they defined themselves and their roles within the family structure. I conclude the chapter with a discussion of the use of regional literature to explore cultural values, issues, and conflicts in people's lives.

Appalachia Within the Southern Context

When we talk about the South as place, we are not referring to one South, but many. Because of the diversity of southern geography and consequent economic situations, several distinct cultural contexts are evident. This is readily seen in a cursory look at the southern literature. William Faulkner, Flannery O'Connor, Maya Angelou, and James Still are all southern writers, yet their stories capture the flavor of a particular geographical region and culture within the broader southern context. The chapters in this volume represent a variety of subcultures within the South. The Appalachian South, certainly part of a larger southern culture, has its own unique geography, history, and culture.

The Appalachian region has been defined differently through the years by social scientists, writers, and politicians. The most recent political definition of Appalachia grew out of efforts to establish the Appalachian Regional Commission (ARC) to address social, educational, and economic concerns of the area. In 1965, the federal government, at the urging of the region's state governors, created the ARC with representatives from thirteen states. This commission divided the region into three distinct subregions: northern, central, and southern Appalachia. By 1970, the total Appalachian region included 397 counties with a population of approximately eighteen million people. Southern Appalachia includes the mountainous portions of Georgia, Mississippi, Alabama, North Carolina, South Carolina, eastern counties of Appalachian Tennessee, and fourteen counties in southwestern Virginia.[1] The Urban Appalachian Council of Cincinnati (1985) defines an Appalachian as one who was born, or whose parents or grandparents were born in one of the counties making up the Appalachian region.

Appalachian Culture

Loyal Jones (1975) in his essay on Appalachian values explains that a strong sense of family, love of the land, independence, self-reliance and pride are of utmost important to Appalachian people. These values are crucial to the maintenance of a sense of freedom. This population, primarily Scotch-Irish, moved to isolated mountain regions where they could be free to enjoy the solitude and beauty of the land, support their families, and live without the constraints of a more populated and therefore, regulated, society. Jones explains that Appalachians value being able to take care of their own without having to depend on others:

> Our forebears were individualistic from the beginning, else they would not have gone to such trouble and danger to get away from encroachments on their freedom. Individualism and self-reliance were traits to be admired on the frontier. The person who could not look after himself and his family was to be pitied. ... The pride of the mountaineer is mostly a feeling of not wanting to be beholden to other people. We are inclined to try to do everything ourselves, find our own way when we are lost on the road, or suffer through when we are in great need. We don't like to ask others for help. The value of self-reliance is often stronger than the desire to get help.[2]

Appalachians identify with place, with their rugged mountains, lush valleys and mountain streams. Their bond to the land is the glue that binds these people to each other and to past generations of Appalachians. It was this mountainous land that initially provided for the Appalachians a subsistence living in the form of crops, game, and wood for heat and shelter. It was a land in which small upland farms could be created in the valleys and hollers in the mountains. In the temperate climate there was an abundance of herbs, grasses, vegetables, nuts, and flowers that grew wild and were readily available. Unlike other parts of the upper South such as that described in Clinton B. Allison's chapter in this volume, this was not land considered desirable by those interested in larger scale farming or access to markets. It was a place in which people could surround themselves with natural beauty while they worked hard to provide their families with a simple living. However, overcrowding of the small farms, exhaustion of the soil, extinction of game, and the discovery of coal in the region have been primary reasons for the Appalachian people's history of economic struggle and exploitation in the twentieth century. Subsequent conflicts between the Appalachian values and the realities of daily survival are the major themes in Appalachian literature. In the following pages, I will explore these themes with illustrations from a sampling of regional novels.

Selected Appalachian Fiction

For the purposes of illustrating cultural themes using Appalachian literature, I selected a variety of novels set in different parts of the region and in different historical periods. Wilma Dykeman's *Tall Woman* (1962) is set in rural Tennessee during the Civil War. Myra Page's *Daughter of the Hills* (1950), James Still's *River of Earth* (1940), and Denise Giardina's *Storming Heaven* (1987) chronicle the rape of the mountains by the coal companies and the impact of mining on the lives of Appalachian families. Harriette Arnow's *Doll-*

maker (1954) depicts the struggles of a rural Kentucky family as they attempt to adjust to life in Detroit during war years of the 1940s. Fred Chappell (1985) in *I am One of You Forever,* set in this same period, uses a World War II tragedy as the focal point in a series of family vignettes that describe one youth's boyhood in rural North Carolina. Lee Smith's *Black Mountain Breakdown* (1980) and *Oral History* (1983) are both set in present-day rural Appalachia. A final novel, Wendall Berry's *The Memory of Old Jack* (1974) recreates the life of a ninety-two year-old man as he reminisces about his years in a small Kentucky river town. The novels I have used for this chapter are merely a sampling of those we used in the course. Many other Appalachian novel for adults and children are available as a base curriculum for cultural study. (See suggested readings preceding notes.)

Although these novels were written at different times about life in various periods, all capture the same cultural themes of Appalachian families. The love of the land with the notion of homeplace serves as the backdrop for all these novels. A strong sense of family and kinship responsibilities is a complimentary theme. This literature allows its students to explore the complexities of lives as Appalachian people attempt to maintain their cultural values in the face of limited economic alternatives, loss of their land, physical danger, and death.

In this chapter, I have chosen to explore several of the role conflicts experienced by Appalachian women. Conflict is the word that most effectively describes the lives of women in much of the literature. These conflicts cannot easily be separated one from another because they are part of a complex whole way of life; they are often interrelated parts of the whole. However, for purposes of discussion, I have pulled them apart so they can be more readily illustrated with portions of the selected novels. Three themes are presented below: (1) The love of the land and constant threat of loss of their homeplace; (2) women's conflict between fulfilling traditional female role expectations and more independent actions based on knowledge of their own strengths and abilities; and (3) conflict between a need for survival in the present and the desire for better education and economic future possibilities for their children.

Love of the Land

The bond with the land provides Appalachians with a sense of peoplehood. The love of the mountains, creeks, hollers, wooded glades, and rocky paths is the core of Appalachian culture. The homeplace provides its people with both beautiful environment in which to live, but also a difficult land in which to survive. The realities of economic survival are constantly weighed against the love of the land for southern mountain people. Denise Giardina (1987) ends *Storming Heaven* with a passage that describes the difficulty of life and even death in the Appalachian mountains:

> It was a tranquil place, but no one could ever imagine a quiet slumber for the dead in that earth. They are not a people made for eternal peace, and even if they were, the mountains would not let them rest. The mountains are conjurers, ancient spirits shaped by magic past time remembered. The dead walk abroad in the shaded coves, or writhe in their graves, punching up with strong arms and legs, waiting for the day.[3]

The pull of the mountains is strong. It may be necessary for Appalachians to leave the hills to make a living, but the mountains continually tug at the heart as a reminder of home. Giardina (1987) beautifully portrays the people's attachment to the mountains in the reflections of one of her main characters, Carrie Bishop:

> I have traveled outside the mountains, but never lived apart from them. I always feared mountains could be as jealous, as unforgiving, as any spurned lover. Leave them and they may never take you back. Besides, I never felt a

need to go. There is enough to study in these hills to last a
lifetime (1987, p. 89).

. . . .

I knew Doc was right. These mountains has got a
powerful pull. They let a man wander so far and then they
yank him back like a fish on a line. I knew Rondal would
sleep uneasy as long as he was away, and the hills would
bring him home.[4]

Lydia McQueen, the central character of Wilma Dykeman's
(1962) *Tall Woman* provides a poignant description of the
way in which this rugged landscape offered escape from the
crowded living conditions of a hillside cabin and a necessary
solitude in which to put into perspective the demands of
daily living:

During the years she had lived up here, Lydia had found in
this rocky crag a deep source of comfort and inspiration.
Its effect on her was something she could not explain and
therefore she had kept it secret to herself. Sometimes on
winter days when the noise of the narrow cabin, congested
with so many people, their laughter and crying, their
walking and running and shuffling, their constant need of
her, seemed to close in with stifling pressure she would
slip out and climb to this precipice. There, standing with
its hard firmness beneath her feet, her head and face
bared to the wind that swept up from the deep valley below and broke in torrents against this ledge, she regained
an inner quiet, a stillness she could not name or identify.
It was an essential to her existence, however—had been
even when she was still a child—as water or food itself.
And as the wind struck her like a wave, taking her breath
for the moment, beating and breaking against her, drown-
ing her in an ocean of air, she was revived. And so she went
back home, but returned to the rock again and again.

. . . .

In the woods and mountains, her orchard and her spring,
Lydia had always found a deep companionship she could
not name or describe. It anchored her, with a firmness and

trueness she scarcely suspected, against the buffeting tides of change, of coming and going, loss and gain.[5]

Nestled in the mountains, many Appalachian families carved out a "homeplace" that remained in their memories despite movement to cities, takeover by mining companies, or financial ruin. The identities of people are anchored in their homeplace; the memories of this place serve as a way to stay connected to the extended family and to the land. The importance of the homeplace is a central theme in much of this literature. In the following excerpt from *Storming Heaven*, a young Carrie Bishop confronts for the first time the feeling of comfort and safety of the homeplace as well as the dangers of the outside world:

> Albion's father came the next week and took him away. I followed their wagon for a time as it trundled up Grapevine toward the ridge that led to the Levisa and West Virginia. Albion was pale and quiet.
>
> "Come on go with us, girl," Thomas Freeman said jovially.
>
> His words were terrible to me. I walked along until we reached the mouth of Scary. Then I stopped. It was the boundary of the Homeplace, a mystical boundary. I feared to cross, feared I would be cast out as Albion was with no place of my own. I waved goodbye, my arm heavy as lead. Albion was a lot to me. I loved him, but it was not enough to hold him. I first began to understand what I have learned since, that there are forces in this world, principalities and powers, that wrench away the things that are loved, people and land, and return only exile.
>
> I ran to the Aunt Jane place to lay my head in the lap of the old woman and weep.[6] (1987, p. 48).

Later in the book, Carrie reflects on the loss of the homeplace, not only as a place to live, but as a place where she and her kin can be buried:

> It was a cold January day. We made biscuits in the kitchen beside a frosted windowpane. Flora flung her arms

around me, careful not to touch me with her flour-dusted
hands. I didn't tell her that I feared we would lose the
Homeplace some day. I tried not to think about it myself.
It was bad enough to dread a long life without the love of
Rondal and hope of children. But if there was no place of
my own to be, no ground where my bones could be laid beside my kin's, would I not be the most miserable creature
in God's world?[7] (1987, p. 129).

Wrenched From the Land

On the reverse side of this deep attachment to the
mountains and the homeplace is the constant threat of its
loss because of economic hardship. Prior to industrialization
at the turn of the century, Appalachian families lived self-
sufficient lives on small farms in the hills. With increased
demand for coal and the takeover of the Appalachian high-
lands by the coal companies, families moved to coal camps to
earn a living. Around 1920, when coal mining was a booming
business, a farmer turned coal miner could buy more in a
week from his earnings than he could grow on a farm in a
year (Still 1978, v–vi). Families were forced from their
homeplaces when the coal companies "bought" the mineral
rights to the land. Demand for coal decreased sharply in the
late 1920s and 1930s leaving many Appalachians landless
and jobless. James Still's *River of Earth,* Denise Giardina's
Storming Heaven, and Myra Page's *Daughter of the Hills* tell
this story.

The promise of work in factories in northern cities of
Detroit, Akron, Cleveland, Dayton, and Cincinnati during
the war years of the 1940s enticed millions of people from
the hills of central and southern Appalachia. Harriette Arnow's *Dollmaker* chronicles this migration. In each of these
novels, the reality of families being wrenched from their
land and homeplace is a dramatic theme. Despite this migration out of the hills, the literature clearly illustrates the
Appalachian's struggle to remain in the mountains or at
least maintain ownership of the homeplace rather than to
move to the mining camps or northern industrial cities in
search of employment.

The struggle to stay on the land depicted in this literature is a conflict primarily for Appalachian women. Men had
no choice. The land would not support their growing families; they believed that employment in coal mines would.
Women of this period were caught between their love for the
homeplace and their obligation as "good wives" to accompany their husbands into the coal camps. They saw themselves as being torn from the homes they loved in the beauty
of the hills and moved to crowded, dusty coal camps where
they would be required to raise their children in small,
poorly constructed company housing. No matter how difficult it was to eke out a living in the mountains, the women
depicted in literature viewed life in coal camps as a cruel
alternative. In addition, this life would insure that their
sons would follow their fathers into the mines. The determination of one woman to stay on her land rather than to
move to a coal camp is illustrated in an angry dialogue between a husband and wife in James Still's *River of Earth:*

> "I had a notion of staying on here," Mother said, her
> voice small and tight. "I'm agin raising chaps in a coal
> camp. Allus getting lice and scratching the itch. I had a
> notion you'd walk of a day to the mine."

> "A far walking piece, a good two mile. Better to get a
> house in the camp."

> "Can't move a garden, and growing victuals."

> "They'll grow without watching. We'll keep them
> picked and dug."

> "I allus had a mind to live on a hill, not sunk in a
> holler where the fog and dust is damping and blacking. I
> was raised to like a lonesome place. Can't get used to a
> mess of womenfolks in and out, borrowing a dab and a
> pinch of this and that, never paying back. Men tromping
> sut on the floors, forever talking brash."

> "Notions don't fill your belly nor kiver your back."

> Mother was on the rag edge of crying. "Forever mov-
> ing yon and back, setting down nowhere for good and all,
> searching for God knows what," she said. "Where air we
> expecting to draw up to?" Her eyes dampened. "Forever

I've wanted to set us down in a lone spot, a place certain and enduring, with room to swing arm and elbow, a garden-piece for fresh victuals, and a cow to furnish milk for the baby. So many places we've lived—the far side one mine camp and next the slay pile of another. Hardburly. Lizzyblue. Tribbey. I'm longing to set me down shorely and raise my chaps proper."

Father's ears reddened. He spoke, a grain angrily. "It was never meant for a body to be full content on the face of this earth. Against my wont it is to be treading the camps, but it's bread I'm hunting, regular bread with a mite of grease on it. To make and provide it's the only trade I know, and I work willing."[8]

In *Storming Heaven,* Carrie Bishop was torn between her love for the homeplace and her desire to be supportive to Rondal, her lifelong lover. She had been living on the family farm while Rondal had been involved in a mineworkers' strike, but came to the coal camp to help out. In contrast to the example above, Rondal was sensitive to her needs and determined to get her to promise to return to the land if he was convicted for his involvement in the strike. He pleads with her to return home:

"Ifn they do [convict him], I want you to promise me you'll go back home. I know how much you love that place. Hit was such a joy to see you git offn that train today, to see the color in your cheeks, and your eyes bright. I know what put the life back in your face."

"Hit was seeing you again."

"No it werent. It was the Homeplace. If they convict, I want you to go back there. I cant bear the thought of being in prison and knowing you're in that tent. I want you back on your land with your people. Promise me, Carrie."

"Only if you promise you'll go back there with me when the strike's over. Leave the coal mines, go back there and be there for good."[9]

For many Appalachians, a return to the land was impossible. Many who had gone north settled permanently in crowded urban neighborhoods made up of other Appalachian family members and friends. They returned to the southern mountains only to visit relatives. Wendall Berry (1974) tells this story through a poignant portrayal of two old women, Nettie and Aunt Fay, as they live out their later years in a strange city far from their beloved mountains:

In the spring, he and Margaret drove to Cincinnati to see Nettie and the old woman, following Nettie's directions to a red brick tenement near the ball park. It was a Sunday afternoon, hot, the streets lined with people sitting out in chairs and on stoops. They entered a dark, stale-smelling building and climbed to the flat that Nettie had rented on the third floor. Nettie was glad to see them, but quiet, uncertain, strange to them suddenly, no longer held to them by any common ground. She missed Port William; she guessed she always would; she liked very well the new people she worked for. But Mat was most touched by the figure of the old woman who was seated in a sort of alcove between a refrigerator and a window that looked out through the iron of the fire escape at the back of another tenement. She seemed shrunken and resigned, her hands emblematically still, lying in her lap. Where was her garden, where were her plants and speckled hens, where were the long paths of her rambles in the pastures and the woods? "Aunt Fanny," he said, "you're a mighty long way from home." "Lord, Mr. Mat," she said, "ain't it the truth!"

. . . .

They didn't stay long. They had come to offer themselves in some way not well understood and had found themselves to be only strangers, useless to the needs of that place. They threaded the crowd of the street back to where they had left their car. Driving home, Mat was full of a fierce sorrow. If he had spoken, he would have wept. If he could have, if they would have come, he would have brought them home. But he knew that his grief went against history, no stranger to him, whose son was dead in the war; he knew there were not even any words to say. And yet he grieved for Nettie and Aunt Fanny, and for the thousands like them, the exiled children of the land to which their history had been a sacrifice. He knew he had seen the end of what deserved to end better than it had.[10]

Strong Appalachian Women and
Traditional Female Roles

The tremendous personal strength of many of the Appalachian women, often in the face of difficult and tragic lives, was a related theme that emerged from our reading of the regional literature. This was a theme that was appreciated and echoed by students in class in their descriptions of their own mothers, aunts, and grandmothers. Berry's (1974) portrayal of Aunt Sam in *I Am One of You Forever* illustrates this strength:

> This was but one of the misfortunes that darkened Aunt Sam's life. When she was seventeen years old and in the middle of her first road tour her father and mother and younger sister had perished in the fire that razed the old homestead in Cherokee County. Her youngest brother had lived on two years in agony before the mercy of his death. The older brother, formerly a brakeman, was paralyzed from a railroad accident. Her grandmother had died when Aunt Sam was a little girl, but her grandfather, at age seventy, had been shot in a boundary line dispute.

> "And look how strong she's stood up under all that," my father said. "She knows how to live with her feelings. When she wants to cry, she just cries right in front of everybody and goes on with her business. When she wants to laugh, she doesn't hold back an inch [11](p. 169).

The literature depicts mountain women as independent, strong and hardworking but also committed to the more traditional female role as caretakers of the family. Women were responsible for maintaining the homeplace, raising a garden, and caring for their children even in their husband's absence. These were necessary roles for women because of the long hours their husbands worked in the mines and factories during much of this century.

Lydia McQueen in *Tall Woman,* Dolly Hawkins in *Daughter of the Hills,* and Gertie Nevels in *The Dollmaker* are all examples of strong Appalachian women who were the anchors for their families. However, despite the social expectations for women in a traditional, patriarchal cultural milieu, the main characters in these novels were able to use their personal abilities and strengths to direct their own lives. All are presented in the novels as empowered individuals who understand their lives and times, yet continue to struggle, to question, to "push back the margins," or to use resistance to try to change undesirable and often inequitable circumstances. In the language of the critical theorists, the strength of human agency is clearly illustrated by these Appalachian women.

Present Realities and Future Possibilities: Struggle for a Better Life

A major struggle for Appalachian women within the family and community was in the education of their children. As depicted in twentieth century literature, they maintained a strong belief that schooling was a way in which their children would be able to "better themselves." A good education would provide a means for their children to get out of the mines and factories—away from poverty. However, this belief in educating children for the future often flew in the face of the present reality that the children were needed to work to help support the family. Economic survival needs, particularly in the first half of the twentieth century, required Appalachian families to use the labor of their children on the land and in the mines. Despite laws to the contrary, children as young as ten years old were taken by their fathers to work in the mines. If taken into the mines, women knew that their boys would no longer be children, but men who would spend most of their lives breathing coal dust. Though usually resigned to this reality, women fought for their children to attend school.

This conflict between a woman's dreams for her children to go to school in order to go beyond the mines and her husband's more immediate needs to have boys at age eleven or twelve go into the mines is clearly portrayed in several of these novels. In Giardina's *Storming Heaven* (1987), a male friend of the family intervened to try to keep one of the young sons from a life in the mines, but was met with opposition from the boy's father. The father insists that the son must contribute to the family's coffers in order for them to survive:

> C. J. Marcum [a friend of the family] used to come visit on Sundays, sit on the front porch with me and sip iced tea he brought up from Annadel.
>
> "One of these days . . . " he was always saying. "One of these days we'll git that land back. One of these days you'll go off to school and come back and help your people." C. J. tried to save me from the mines. It was like him to think that he could. Daddy started taking me with him when I was ten. The law said you had to be fourteen, but the company looked the other way. Daddy thought if I helped, he might get out of debt to the company store. C. J. came down to argue with him.
>
> "They aint never going to let you out of debt," he said. "The bastards is weighing you light as it is. They'll keep right on no matter how much coal that boy loads."
>
> "It will help," Daddy insisted. "Denbigh says hit could mean as much as fifty cent more a day. And he's taking Talcott on as a breaker. We'll do a lots better."
>
> "What about Rondal's schooling?"
>
> "What about it? He cant eat them books."
>
> "He could be a lawyer or a doctor someday."
>
> "Someday. You're a-talking twenty year down the road about something might as well be a fairy story. Boy aint smart enought for that."
>
> "That boy is plenty smart. You just aint around to see it. They got you stuck in that hole so you dont know what's going on in the world."

"Damn it, C. J., I know what it takes to live. Look at my woman. She aint nothing but skin and bones. She dont eat no supper half the time sos the younguns can have some. Schooling takes money, and I aint got none. Have you?"

My heart sank when C. J. shook his head.[12]

After Rondal and his younger brother Talcott began to work in the mines with their father, their mother's frustration, fear, and despair are painfully described:

When we left the mine at the end of the day I was so weary from shoveling coal that I could not walk very fast. When we came for Talcott, he could not stand up, but sat hunched over on his bench. Daddy picked him up and he cried out.

"Dont worry, son," Daddy said. "You'll git toughened up."

I heard Mommy crying in the kitchen that night before I slept.

"What am I supposed to do? I'm a-scairt to hug my own babies for fear of hurting them. I seen bruises all over Talcott's back where that boss man hit on him. Aint no mother supposed to let such things happen to her younguns."

"Shut up!" Daddy said. "I can take care of them boys."

I closed my eyes.[13] (p. 24).

When it was time for her last son to be taken into the coal mines, the mother refused to allow her husband to do so:

"Yall aint taking my boy down in that hole."

Kerwin stood by the stove and stirred a pot of soup.

"Talcott loaded a heap of coal," Daddy said wearily.

"This boy cant load no coal. He's too skinny. Look at him. Jesus has set his mark on him. You cant have this boy."

"Mommy, we aint said we was taking him in."

She rounded on me. "Nor dont you think you will, neither."

"That damn Talcott," Daddy said. "Why'd he do such a durn fool thing?"

"I don't mind going in," Kerwin said in a small voice. "The Lord will watch over me. Aint it so, Mommy?"

She started to cry. "

"You aint going in," I said.[14] (p. 77).

Later, when the need for mineworkers had diminished and the factories of the North were trying to meet wartime needs, Appalachian women struggled to keep their sons out of the military and away from the factories. A poignant quote from Gertie, the main character in Harriette Arnow's *The Dollmaker* (1954) illustrates the bitterness of this struggle:

"What crops do they raise in this country?" the [police] officer asked, as if he didn't much care but wanted to make some sound above the child's breathing.

"A little uv everthing."

"But what is their main crop?" he insisted.

"Youngens," she said, holding the child's hands that were continually wandering toward the hole in his neck. "Youngens fer the wars an them factories."[15] (pp.24–25).

Appalachian women who were successful at providing their children with more promising futures through a "good education" were then faced with the possible consequences of that education. Schooling does enable their children to escape the mines and factories, but also takes them away from home and perhaps away from the Appalachian cultural values and beliefs. Lee Smith (1980) illustrates this point:

Like a lot of people around Black Rock who never had one, Lorene has great faith in the power of what she calls a "good education," not realizing yet that the children you work so hard to send out will probably never come back, or will come back all changed and ashamed of you, with new ideas of their own.[16]

Wendall Berry (1974) captures this conflict between the value of education for a more prosperous future and the accompanying loss of a beloved past:

> It was only a week ago, when Henry left Port William and went back to Hargrave to begin his own last year of high school, that Andy felt himself borne irrevocably toward the future that is so dark and questionable to him. He stayed on with Mat and Margaret, working in the tobacco harvest, but now there lay in him a strange sorrow that seemed not to go away even when he was thoughtless of it or asleep. And when he put his mind to it he knew what it was: it was the fear that in order to be what he might become he would have to cease to be what he had been, he would have to turn away from that place to which his flesh and his thoughts and devotion belonged. For it was the assumption of much of his schooling, it was in the attitude of most of his teachers and schoolmates, it was in the bearing of history toward such places as Port William and even Hargrave, that achievement, success, all worthy hope lay elsewhere, in cities, in places of economic growth and power; it was assumed that a man must put away his origin as a childish thing.[17]

Ironically, the very education Appalachian mothers struggle to provide for their children, in addition to enabling them to pursue a more comfortable lifestyle, may also distance them from their cultural roots.

Discussion

What does this examination of the cultural themes in Appalachian literature contribute to a discussion on the sig-

nificance of place in the curriculum? In both undergraduate
and graduate teacher education programs, students are provided with a few opportunities to study sociocultural aspects
of schooling. These understandings are generally presented
in social foundations courses that tend to comprise a slim
portion of the total teacher education program. At the undergraduate level these courses are surveys in which students are merely exposed to the study of education through
philosophical, historical, and sociological perspectives. At the
graduate level, students may take one or two courses in history, sociology, anthropology, or philosophy of education. It is
possible for students to move through an entire teacher education program with only minimal understandings of sociocultural aspects of the schools and the communities in
which they will teach. It is rare for teacher education students to take courses in which they examine their own sociocultural backgrounds and the ways in which these
backgrounds and the ways in which these backgrounds have
molded their theories about schooling. It is even rarer for
these students to examine ways in which the sociocultural
context in which their students live may be used in the design and implementation of school curriculum.

In designing the "Schooling in Appalachia" course, I
wanted students to have experiences that would encourage
them to explore their own cultural backgrounds and those of
their students. In addition, I hoped that this type of exploration would provide them with new ways to interact with students and allow them to glimpse alternative curricular
possibilities.

As I reflect on our experiences in that class, it is clear
that the use of Appalachian literature was essential for the
students to become engaged in the complexities and conflicts of life in Appalachia. They found themselves and their
families in these stories. As a result of their reading and
class discussions, students reached out to parents, grandparents, aunts, and uncles for stories and family histories.
One woman interviewed her mother, grandmother, and great
uncle, all Appalachian educators, about their experiences in
mountain schools. She concluded her final paper:

My background in teaching is as strong as is my Appalachian background. I believe that some day, in the future, I shall return to the teaching profession. My grandmother's love of the drama was recreated in me; my mother's drive and determination have been passed on to me; and my great-uncle's practical approach to problem solving is beginning to come my way, too. I am an Appalachian, born and bred.[18]

Another student summarized what she had learned about her own family:

The family to which I belong fits some of the researched data but not all. The stream migration patterns, the one and two-room schooling, the love of place and desire to move "back home," the family solidarity and high moral standards are all exhibited in this group. There are exceptions, also. Some members are more educated than the norm, some have experienced positive attitudes from their northern co-workers. Some have moved farther away from home than others. However, I see more of the "typical" Appalachians than the exceptional. This picture is one of which I can be proud. We native Appalachians, despite all adversity, are an interesting and unique group of people.[19]

Through fiction, these students were able to capture their own past and present through their emotions as well as their intellects. They came to class excited at the similarities between characters in the novels and themselves. The course allowed us to "engage our hearts as well as our minds" (Shaker & Kridel 1989).

Other Suggested Appalachian Readings:

Agee, James. *A Death in the Family.* Boston: Houghton Mifflin, 1969.

Carter, Forrest. *The Education of Little Tree.* Albuquerque: University of New Mexico Press, 1976.

Dykeman, Wilma. *The Far Family.* New York: Holt, Rinehart, 1966.

Fox, John, Jr. *The Trail of the Lonesome Pine.* 1908. Reprint. Lexington, KY: University Press of Kentucky, 1984.

Giles, Janice Holt. *Miss Willie* Boston: Houghton Mifflin, 1953.

Haun, Mildred. *The Hawk's Done Gone and Other Stories.* 1940. Reprint. University Press, 1968.

Higgs, Robert J. and Manning, Ambrose N. *Voices from the Hills: Selected Readings of Southern Appalachia.* New York: Ungar, 1975.

McCarthy, Cormack. *The Orchard Keeper.* New York: Random House, 1965.

Marius, Richard. *The Coming of Rain.* New York: Alfred Knopf, 1969.

Marshall, Catherine. *Christy.* New York: McGraw-Hill, 1967.

Norman, Gurney. *Divine Right's Trip: A Folk Tale.* New York: Dial Press, 1972.

Still, James. *Run for the Elbertas.* 1936. Reprint. Lexington, KY: University Press of Kentucky, 1980.

Stuart, Jesse. *Men of the Mountains.* 1941. Reprint. Lexington, KY: University Press of Kentucky, 1979.

Stuart, Jesse. *Trees of Heaven.* 1940. Reprint. Lexington, KY: University Press of Kentucky, 1979.

Wolfe, Thomas. *Look Homeward, Angel: A Story of the Buried Life.* New York: Scribner, 1929.

Part III

Elements of Race

5

Willie Morris and the Southern Curriculum: Emancipating the Southern Ghosts

——————————— *Joe L. Kincheloe* *

In his speculations on the nature of a curriculum theory of southern studies, William Pinar draws upon the various strands of research that have informed reconceptualized curriculum theorizing. Grounded in critical theory and psychoanalysis, the southern curriculum is dedicated to a *social* psychoanalysis aided by the methodologies of historiography, ethnography, phenomenology, gender studies, autobiography, and literary criticism. In many ways Willie Morris brings together these approaches to southern studies in his corpus of work on his South.

Morris's nonfiction draws upon historiographical and ethnographic traditions. His autobiographical sensitivity is innocently phenomenological, as he responds poetically to the southern ghosts that haunted his mind and body. His work is permeated with references to the process by which gender role is fashioned in the South. These references are sometimes presented consciously, other times they are uncovered only by gender sensitive readers who discover manifestations of gender role formation by interrogating that psychic realm that is evidently not conscious to the author himself and is determined by subtle social conditioning. For a plethora of reasons, the work of Willie Morris is valuable in the reconceptualized southern curriculum.

Morris's work is primarily autobiographical, constantly relating his personal story to the story of his place. He carries on a grand southern literary convention: The writer's exploration of the southern traditions and his or her attempt to document the personal struggle to come to terms with those traditions in his or her own life. Morris is a student of the southern traditions, and the southern mythologies—he understands their variations, their nuances, and their death throes. He moves easily among the structures and codes of southern literature, invoking the vocabularies that were used by his literary ancestors without self-consciousness. As the twentieth century with its interstate highways and McDonald's mute the old voices, Morris seems determined to pour through the family album one more time before consigning it to the attic. His work is a eulogy—the interment will follow.

By the time Morris published his first book *North Toward Home* in 1967, the journalistic motif of Southerner-in-struggle had fossilized. The ghosts had done their job well. The liberal sons and daughters of the South found themselves without a home, their small towns and cities haunted by the specters of racism, violence, and poverty. Critics sometimes blasted Morris's work for its stylized quality—Faulkner without the urgency. While such criticisms hold some truth, they miss some important aspects of Morris's work and place in southern literary history. Morris writes of structures of feelings that are no longer his; he utilizes literary conventions whose rules have been determined not by his but previous generations. The homage he pays to the southern memories is self-consciously temporary—tomorrow, we feel, Morris must move on to the business of the present. Today, however, he is showing his kids "how it was" when he grew up. Indeed, Willie Morris is the weigh station between Faulkner and postmodernist southern writer, Barry Hannah, the movement from Southern League baseball to Lynyrd Skynyrd, from moonshine to cocaine.

Faulkner was truly a regional writer. No doubt, he challenged the myths, but the myths still held the imagination. The modernist tendencies that Faulkner expressed were couched in southern terms. Where Faulkner's work is of the South in a particular place and time, Morris finds his influences outside the temporal and spatial boundaries of Yoknapatawpha. Morris's South is lost to him: he is no longer a small town Southerner (though he eventually moves back to Oxford, Mississippi); and his land is lost to itself as the myths fade away from memory.

This analysis of Morris concerns itself with emancipation or liberation, the diversity of its expression, and the peculiar textures of southern life as they relate to the concept of liberation. We are all familiar by now with the discourse of emancipation, its poetic tone, and its dangerous implications for the preservers of the status quo. We understand its attempt to render problematic that which had previously been accepted as given, and its exhortation to reflect upon the essence of that which before had only been considered in terms of its use, its instrumental value. More and more educators have come to realize that liberation embodies a form of rationality that involves the capacity to think about thinking (Gouldner 1976).

Emancipation has come to be seen as praxis, that is, an understanding of the ways in which human beings are dominated as well as forms of actions that serve to counter dominating forces (Giroux 1981). Emancipation involves a form of critical thinking that moves us beyond common sense assumptions into a new territory marked by an understanding of genesis and purpose (McLaren 1989). In our new dialectical mode, we see past isolated events, as we begin to think in terms of processes. Thus, emancipatory thinking allows individuals to participate in the sociohistorical transformation of their society, as they begin to bring their work under their own control (Freire 1985).

In our attempt to understand the conventions of our place and how they have shaped us, we engage in what William Pinar and I, in our introduction label "social psychoanalysis." This social psychoanalysis may be referred

to as "critical historiography." Emerging from a critical theoretical tradition this social psychoanalysis/critical historiography is an essential feature of southern curriculum
theorizing. Jurgen Habermas considers Freudian psychoanalysis a model for a critical science, for it is only psychoanalysis that serves as an example of a science
incorporating a methodical process of self-reflection (Habermas 1970).

As the psychoanalyst attempts to remedy the mystified
self-perceptions of the analysand, the social psychoanalyst
sees myth invalidation as an important step toward social
progress (Held 1980). Such an attempt, just like the effort of
the psychoanalyst to confront patients with actual forces
that helped shape their psyches, is thwarted by many factors: for example, the success of the logic of capital in
late industrial societies in reifying existing social, political,
and economic relationships; and the psychological distortions of past racial, gender, and social class role definitions
in say southern culture. In the modern industrialized South,
both of these prementioned factors may work in concert cre-
ating a symphony of unique distortions (Marcuse 1964; Marcuse 1978).

The power of such distortions on the individual and social level is undeniable—history is frozen and viewed as rational, as if it could be no other way (Jacoby 1975). Until
free people invalidate the myths and conceive of the possibilities offered by emancipation, slim is the possibility of authentic self-direction on the individual and social levels. The
less social and individual self-direction which exists, the
more it appears that society is governed by rational and intractable natural laws (Marcuse 1960). This is the concern of
the reconceptualized southern curriculum—to demystify
southern experience in such a manner that distortions are
confronted. In this way southern consciousness can be rene-
gotiated with all participants—especially those previously
excluded at the bargaining table. Such an undertaking allows for a language of possibility (Giroux and McLaren
1989). The southern ghosts, who siphon their energy from

the frozen history of race, class, and gender, find themselves exposed—they can no longer haunt with anonymity.

Myth

Our discussion of social distortion—especially in the context of literature—cannot proceed without an examination of a Barthesian notion of myth. Roland Barthes reflects Marcuse's concern with the existence of natural and rational law as he focuses his notion of semiology on myth. Myth, Barthes argues, provides a *natural* image of reality, as it ignores the existence of the dialectical relationship between activities and human actions. Myth renders such activities "a harmonious display of essences." Barthes contends that myth in talking about things, purifies them, makes them innocent, gives them a natural and eternal justification. Myth, he continues:

> abolishes the complexity of human acts, it gives them the simplicity of essences, it does away with all dialectics, with any going back beyond what is immediately visible, it organizes a world which is without contradictions because it is without depth, a world wide open and wallowing in the evident, it establishes a blissful clarity: things appear to mean something by themselves.[1]

Thus, the historical quality of things is lost. When myth conquers, individuals lose the memory that things were once made. As a complicated network of arguments, beliefs, and metaphors, myths become the vehicles through with societies deny historical origin and in the process support and authenticate their identities. Richard Gray writes that it is the recovery of the memory that Barthes is talking about here—"that things were once made"—that separates good southern literature from the mediocre (Gray 1986, p. 272). For example, Faulkner demanded that we examine the codes and the hidden structures that grant insight into myth etiology. As Gray puts is, Faulkner "offers an examination of the way the world has been placed into words" (Gray, 272).

The myths of the South are great deceivers. The Patriarchal Myth of a cultural gentry with a superior notion of civilization, the Lost Cause Myth with its implicit justification of the Civil War aims, the Myth of Southern Womanhood with its glorification of feminine passivity, the Myth of the Happy Darkie on the benevolent plantation, the Gentlemanly Code of Honor Myth with its frozen notion of masculinity all claim to be drawing upon history, centering human action historically. The myths are charlatans, reifying the status quo, presenting themselves as an accurate account of the essence of things. In providing answers to our southern identity search, the myths simplify and "explain" our origins. The only way to maintain our identity is via myth invocation and imitation—a process that Southerners have mastered over the decades, especially through their literature.

Myths may be used in a variety of ways. Political demagogues may employ the myth manipulatively to create allegiance to practices and symbols that serve the interest of the demagogue. Myths may be used innocently, as they are every day, to make sense of the world around us, to provide certainty in the chaotic lived world, In a critical sense myths may be employed by the demystifier. Like Claude Levi-Strauss, the demystifier may accomplish the task of deciphering the myth for all to see; or the demystifier may seek to locate the myth historically and understand the social forces that contributed to its sanctification. Whatever the process or combination of processes, the act of demystification is an act of social psychoanalysis as it uncovers the existence of social distortion, its genesis, its nature, and its effects. Curriculum theory grounded in social psychoanalysis and place is informed by Barthesian myth analysis and the subsequent process of demystification and myth explication.

The demystification process necessitates a well-developed sense of the past—a sense that must distinguish between history and myth. Traditionally preoccupied with the past, Southerners must draw upon their non-mythical historical sense to overcome the malformations of the present. Southern writer William Humphrey describes the historical sense of the region, arguing that: "If the Civil War is more alive to the Southerner than the Northerner it is because all the past is." Colonel Sartaris in Faulkner's *Flags in the Dust* (and many of his other characters as well) is so overpowered by things past that he seems pale in their reflection. In some ways, Willie Morris appears as a Faulknerian character in his own autobiographical writing—so powerful are his ghosts. Certainly this historical sense has begun to fade in the fast food, TV age. Contrary to more sanguine interpretations, the social amnesia that attends this fading does not destroy the myths. The mythological foundations of southern society remain intact—indeed, they are rendered more impervious to challenge—as the fading memory is accompanied by the fading of possibility. The southern curriculum must draw sustenance from this traditional southern sense of the past.

Faulkner recognized the possibility of memory. The past was never seen as inert or buried but as a living presence always capable of growth (Gray 1986, p. 181). Along with Robert Penn Warren and Allen Tate, Faulkner recognized the dialectical interaction between past and present—a recognition carried on by Willie Morris in *North Toward Home* and maybe most profoundly in *The Courting of Marcus Dupree*. This dialectical relationship involves alteration on both sides of the coin. Tate's "Ode to the Confederate Dead" examines a man in crisis standing in a Confederate graveyard. As he imagines what the lives of those buried there were like, he measures his failure against them. The ghosts are there, but they are the ghosts of the man's own invention—he constructs them with the bits of evidence available. The existence of *Tradition,* an ossified mythology, is not assumed in the poem. Tate's concern is that tradition doesn't merely exist, it is made. His character is making tradition, reinventing the past. Not only, the reader is reminded, does the past shape the present, but the present also shapes the past. The dialectic is celebrated, possibility is restored (Tate 1970, p. 18). R. G. Collingwood reflected this idea of the human construction of the past when he wrote that all history is the reenactment of the past through the mind of the his-

torian. We are not passive beings who surrender to the spell
of others' interpretations of the past, to the spell of *Tradition*. History, he concluded, is an active process, a reenactment of past thought. The reenactment takes place in the
context of the historian's own knowledge (Collingwood, 1962,
pp. 215, 242-43).

We must become our own storytellers, Eudora Welty
states. Nothing ever happens once and is finished, the past
lives on. As Southerners tell their stories, enhance their reputations as raconteurs, they construct their individual versions of the past. Welty, too, views history as a dialectical
process—an interchange between the "out there" (the objective) and the "in here" (the subjective). Each time a story is
told there is a reweaving of facts—some details are omitted,
some reemphasized. Tradition is challenged, the presentation of past as myth is overcome.

The southern victimization by Tradition takes many
forms. Morris documents the power of the southern myths to
evoke unquestioned allegiance from his fellow delta dwellers. Was it the power of the myths that elicited such zealous
support from the poor and non-slaveholding South that individuals were willing to give their lives to protect a "peculiar
Institution" that certainly did not serve their economic interests? Erich Fromm examines this southern phenomenon
psychoanalytically. Using Freud's notion of narcissism,
Fromm develops a theory of social narcissism to explain the
tendency of some suppressed classes to be loyal to their social superiors and their rulers.

For an organized group to survive, it is important that
the members of the group possess narcissistic energy. The
members must consider the group as important or even
more important than their own lives. Fromm labels the social narcissism benign if it is based on pride in a great
achievement. It is malignant, he contends, if it is based not
on something the group has produced but on something it
has, for example, its splendor, its past achievements, its skin
color, its code of gentlemanly behavior, and so forth. . . . For
those who are economically poor and socially excluded, narcissistic pride in belonging is an important source of satis-

faction. Since their confined existence evokes little outlet for interest and little possibility for various forms of mobility, they may develop an exaggerated form of narcissism. The most extreme form of southern racism has traditionally come from the lower middle classes as its members view themselves as superior to the "inferior" Blacks, for example, the Bourbon protection of Blacks from lower middle-class Whites in post-Reconstruction era, the lower middle class following of George Wallace in the late 1960s and early 1970s.

> Even though I am poor and uncultured, I am somebody important because I belong to the most admirable group in the world—I am White.[2]

Thus, Southerners must escape the ravages of Tradition and the psychic mutilations it carries with it. Critical theoretical analysis with its discomfort with surface explanations offers hope.

Paulo Friere extends our thinking about the relationship between these psychic mutilations, historical location, anthropological context, and liberation. Arguing for a liberatory education, which frees humans from the oppression that traps in the web their historical reality, Freire ponders the *risk* of their emancipation. "Existence is not despair, but risk," he tells us. Those who seek liberation must risk themselves, though the "form of the risk" will vary from individual to individual and from place to place. The liberatory risk of a Brazilian is quite different from that of a Swiss; indeed, the liberatory risk of a New Yorker is quite different from that of a Mississippian. Our sociohistorical context shapes the form of our risk. The attempt to universalize the form and content of the liberating risk is ill-advised and unacceptable, Freire posits, to anyone who thinks dialectically.

Children of the Southern Place

I am a child of the South, one who had sought to understand the rhythms of southern life and their effects on me.

For many reasons, my first exposure to Willie Morris about twenty years ago provided much insight into my own *southern* consciousness. So profound was the effect that I adopted Morris's *North Toward Home* for my introduction to education classes when I came to Louisiana to teach. An excellent educational autobiography, I hoped that the work would touch the consciousness of my students. I hoped that it would promote an introspective analysis of personal educational experience that might lead to a better understanding of the social forces that shaped southern students.

Emerging from the Yazoo City, Mississippi of the 1940s and early 1950s, Willie Morris chronicles his journey from a small town provencial to New York editor of *Harper's* to writer in residence at the University of Mississippi. Haunted by the power of Yazoo (even the sound of the word conjures ghosts), Morris struggles to comprehend the sway of the South in his life. Never far away from the consciousness of the southern sense of place, Morris presents a corpus of work that sheds light on the nature of liberation, its ambiguity, and its contextual contingency.

"Where are you from?" the Mississippian asked.

"What do you mean?"

"Well, where are you from? Where did you go to high school?"

The other man mentioned an Eastern prep school.

"But where did you grow up? Where are your parents?"

"Well, my father is in Switzerland, I think, and my mother is asleep in the next room."[3]

Morris reports this conversation between a young Mississippian and a Harvard man. Awakened by the traumatic interchange the Mississippian confides: "For the first time in my life, I understood that not all Americans are *from* somewhere." I think of myself as a teacher on the first day of class calling the roll and asking each student where they are from—somehow it is important as I match names with faces and attempt to learn something about them. To those from the small rural towns and parishes around Shreveport it is a natural question, and they talk with ease about life in Vivian, Greenwood, Plain Dealing, or Cotton Valley; to others, it is a strange, irrelevant question and they dismiss it—sometimes not even attempting an answer.

So strong is the southern awareness of place that when people from different towns meet they talk at length not only about where they are from but also where their parents are from. More often than not, the stranger will know exactly the location of the little hometowns. I know intimately the terrain and the now long dead personalities of my parents' original homes in Bland, Virginia, and Hawkins County, Tennessee. For Southerners, Thorton Wilder wrote, "place, environment, relation, repetitions are the breath of their being." It is the charge of each Southerner to work out the power of *place* in his or her own existence (Morris 1983b).

While Southerners have traditionally found themselves divided by lines of race, class, and gender, a sense of ambivalence (a sense that frustrates attempts to generalize about the South) renders such divisions problematic. This elusive southern consciousness of place seems to cut across racial and class lines, forming a tacit alliance between the South's professors, journalists, Black preachers, and hot rodders with Confederate flags on their rear bumpers. Indeed, both Black preachers and Klansmen agree that "the South is a good place to raise children" (Yoder 1967). Morris recollects that during his exile in New York, he shared far more understanding with Black Mississippians than with the Yankee Wasps he met daily (Morris 1967). *North Toward Home* is filled with references to his friendship with Black authors and fellow southern expatriates, Al Murray and Ralph Ellison. On New Year's Day 1967, Morris describes their feast at Al Murray's apartment in Harlem of bourbon, collard greens, black-eyed peas, ham hocks, and cornbread—the traditional southern New Year's Day good luck dinner (p. 387). These southern connections are complex and often incomprehensible to outsiders. Consider C. Vann Woodward's recollections of his thoughts while marching with Martin Luther King on the road to Montgomery: "I looked to the side of the road, and I saw the red-necks lined up, hate all over their faces, distrust and misunderstanding in their eyes. And I'll have to admit something. A little part of me was there with them" (Woodward, 399).

The Ghosts

The struggle for emancipation for the Southerner is thus a complex enterprise inhabited by a potpourri of regional ghosts. *Morris ponders the mindless racism, the origins of the acts of violence he and his boyhood friends committed against isolated Black children.*

Hiding in the shrubbery, twelve-year-old Willie watched a young Black girl and her little brother walk down a deserted Yazoo sidewalk.

> The older girl walked by first, and the child came along a few yards behind. Just as he got in front of me, lurking there in the bushes, I jumped out and pounced on him. I slapped him across the face, kicked him with my knee, and with a shove, sent him sprawling on the concrete.[4]

Morris saw this violent display as more than a mere gratuitous act of childhood cruelty: "It was something else, infinitely more subtle and contorted." Blacks were always viewed ambivalently by the Yazoo Whites. "They were always ours to do with as we wished" with their degenerate lifestyles and distasteful habits. Dirty Whites "kept house like a nigger"; a "nigger car" was dilapidated and didn't run well; staying out all night and being seen with a variety of male companions made a woman guilty of "nigger behavior"; and conversation filled with lies and superstition was "nigger talk." Yet, despite all of this, Whites harbored a vague feeling for a mutual past with Blacks—a bond of shared place.[5]

He relives the religious tyranny, the public school teachers and the Sunday School "church ladies" who imposed a Christianity by fear and rote.

As a fourth grader, Willie found himself entrusted to public school teacher Miss Abbott and her white-bearded, king of clubs, American sympathizing anthropomorphic God. Miss Abbott passed along God's pronouncements on the niggers and the Japs while the children of Yazoo spent a good portion of their mornings memorizing and reciting Bible verses. The lessons, buoyed by the omnipresent threat of hell, were not lost on the Yazoo youth. "Our fundamentalism was so much a part of us that its very sources, even its most outrageous gyrations and circumlocutions, went unquestioned." So unchallenged was the Yazoo fundamentalism that Willie and his friends would go near the local Catholic Church only when they were taunted and dared. Knowledge of the exact nature of God's will was rarely deemed problematic and was used to arrest the impulses of Willie and his adolescent peers.[6]

He describes the important struggle for the honor of being a "good old boy," marked by self-conscious anti-intellectualism and male bonding rituals.

Nothing was more important than good old boyism. In the presence of one's males peers, it was incumbent that the good old boy exhibit a well-cultivated cynicism about academic concerns. A boy's real friends, those among whom he felt comfortable being himself, were to be found in the male peer group, for association with popular and attractive girls was not pursued merely for its intrinsic worth—such associations brought with them increased status in the male group.[7]

He writes of an elementary and high school education divorced from reality, a ritual so obsessed with form that knowledge of the outside world or knowledge of self was consciously repressed.

I read the books, Morris writes, to stay on the good side of the teachers and to get A's, but they meant nothing to me and made no impact on the way I lived or saw experience. "I didn't understand my own intelligence ... I was extraordinarily dependent on the judgment of my elders. ... All the things I wrote and read in high school I relegated to the farther crevices of my mind." High school was a preparation for entry into educated land gentry of Mississippi; it was designed to conform sensibilities to the needs of such a life not to understand its origins and contradictions. The Yazoo schools had left Morris ignorant of himself and the "world of moving objects" he was about to enter. Had he understood that great books "were for one's own private soul rather than mere instrumentalities for achieving those useless trinkets on which all American high schools . . . base their existence" maybe he would have better understood the delta ghosts:

> . . . perhaps I would have found in Faulkner some dark chord, some suggestion of how this land had shaped me, how its isolation and its guilt-ridden past had already settled so deeply into my bones.[8]

He reconstructs a southern middle-class enculturation, a process that explicitly delineated what exactly constituted the dominant cultural capital and the specific ways it was to be acquired.

All the middle-class kids in Yazoo tacitly understood that they would make it through school all right, someday becoming the leaders of the community—the planters, store owners, druggists, and lawyers. We were the ones, Morris writes, who "read faster and better than the slower children of the families from 'out in the country' . . . we knew we were the teachers' favorites; we knew that the stirring challenges they laid down were secretly meant only for us" (Morris 20–21). Morris' first months as a student at the University of Texas were merely an extension of the quest for cultural capital. Surrounded by fraternity men in search of fun and status, Morris received sartorial advice and harsh criticism about his table manners (Morris, 151). Joining a number of organizations, Morris was comforted by the assurance of his social success.

> Versatility, gregariousness, the social graces, these were the important things, just as they had been in Yazoo;

these were what the University of Texas could provide only bigger and better.[9]

He reflects on his familiarity with an intense sense of belonging to Yazoo, a comfort that was sufficiently powerful to crush the latent, shadowy desire of his friends and acquaintances to go beyond it.

It was a land that elicited love, Morris tells us (Morris 1981). The sense of community that persists ties everything to everything else, everybody to everybody else. "Everything makes waves," Neshoba County scholar-in-residence Seena Kohl observed (Morris 1983b). Morris saw his place in Yazoo; he imagined marrying his majorette, buying his land, and settling into the warm southern comfort. What more could there possibly be, he only occasionally wondered. After a Saturday night of high school partying at the house of some Yazoo parents who had traveled to Oxford for the Old Miss football game, Morris was satisfied.

I was with the little plantation girl I loved, and old friends who had been friends for as long as I could remember in a town as familiar and settled to me as anything I would ever know, I would never wander very far away.[10]

Along with these regional ghosts exists an omnipresent sense of trauma in the southern upbringing, a blood and darkness which, on the one hand, obviously crushes the emancipatory impulse, but, on the other hand, provides a fertile ground for its cultivation. Morris refers to this thought as "the grace of character gained through suffering and loss." Could it be the "dialectic of place?" Does liberation require trauma? The tyrannies of southern life are all too real: its shattered dreams, the failures of its history, the insights gained from living with a great human wrong, and an "un-American" poverty (Morris 1981). Liberation, I believe, *does* require myth confrontation. Morris the high school senior was comfortable with the Patriarchal Myth with its notions of gentility and a superior civilization. The existence of the tyrannies of southern life simply did not fit the myth;

thus, consciousness of the tyrannies was repressed and the party continued.

Such realities provide Southerners the possibility of a unique vantage point (I see it in my students) from which they may come to understand their own history, American history in general, and the irony of modern affluent America (Morris 1967). The ghosts won't let us forget. With its historical sense ever close to the surface, the South holds the possibility of memory with all of the subversive power memory provides. A sense of history allows us to understand the traditions that have formed our autobiographies and the textures of our intersubjective relationships (Giroux 1981). Recognizing the sources of suffering in our past, we are empowered to initiate a discourse that refuses to assume that the present has been naturally or rationally constructed (Freire and Macedo 1987).

The southern historical consciousness has been profoundly touched by the omnipresence of Black culture. Marked by an interesting dialectic of political, economic, and social marginality on one hand and cultural power on the other, Blacks represent the South's blood and darkness. The Black man and woman are compelling emblems of Original Sin. In Faulkner's *Go Down Moses,* young Roth Edmonds realizes that he can no longer sleep beside Henry Beauchamp, the Black boy who had been his closest friend. There was no specific event that motivated Roth's decision, Faulkner writes. Just one day the old curse of his fathers came down on him; he inherited the racial prejudice and guilt of his ancestors. Hence, he reenacts their Original Sin in his own life (Faulkner 1960, 91). William Styron's Stingo in *Sophie's Choice* is another inheritor of southern Original Sin as he fights with the guilt derived from his awareness that he is the progeny of the slaveholders and has profited at whatever distance from the buying and selling of human flesh (Styron 1980, 249).

Morris is aware of the power of this historical consciousness—an impulse that by its nature creates that sense of critical distance necessary to emancipation. There is a painful quality to the distance necessary to liberation, and Morris with his southern sense of the tragic is drawn to it. To really understand a place in one's heart, he laments, "his heart must remain subtly apart from it." The liberated Southerner must "always be a stranger to the place he loves, and its people." While he may be shaped by the historical sense of the southern place and recognize the beauties within it, he knows that there are too many ghosts to embrace it completely. "He must absorb without being absorbed" (Morris 1981). Faulkner understood this axiom on a variety of levels. Oxford, Mississippi was Faulkner's expertise but it could not ever completely become his home. Richard Gray argues that Faulkner could only half enter it. Alternately in love with it and offended by it (again the dialectic place?), Faulkner had to pull back. His stories are authored by a double agent, "an insider and outsider" (Gray 1986, 171). Standing on the football field at Philadelphia (Mississippi) High School with legendary running back Marcus Dupree, Willie Morris listened to this untraveled, Black high school football star talk about how much he wanted to stay in Mississippi. Reflecting back on the ghosts, Morris told Dupree: "Sometimes we have to leave home, Marcus, before we can really come back" (Morris 1983b).

But what moved Willie himself to leave Mississippi is not exactly clear to him. There were fleeting awarenesses of worlds other than Yazoo. Reading Booth Tarkington's *Seventeen* in high school study hall set the stage of an "out of mind" experience:

> I gazed out the window and lazily soaked in the soft spring afternoon, and all of a sudden I felt overcome for no reason at all by the likelihood of a great other world somewhere out there—of streamlined express trains and big cities, and boats sailing to other countries; the teacher snapped, "Willie, get back to that book!"[11]

Morris is haunted by the attempt to uncover the genesis of his desire to leave Mississippi. What constituted the abrasive grain of sand in his perception of things that scratched hidden ambitions and stirrings of independence? Though never exactly sure, Morris attributes his desire to remove himself from his deepest loyalties to his imagination. It was his imagination that held his will hostage when he was commissioned to write the prophecy of the Class of 1952 of Yazoo High School. His presentation of an irreverent, harshly satirical projection of the fate of his classmates elicited an angry response from his previously adoring teachers. You might as well leave here, one teacher told him, "because it's pretty clear that you don't appreciate the people around you" (Morris, 144). His imagination was beginning to formulate a vision of life beyond the honor roll, popularity, and the comforts of delta life. The limitations of a life that focused on delta courtesies and delta manners were slowly becoming apparent; indeed, a deeper level of human understanding was possible. The word may have been unfamiliar to the graduating senior, but Morris was in the first stages of the search of his *Lebenswelt*.

Though he possessed a latent potential for liberation, Morris did little to expand the envelope of his consciousness in his first months at the University of Texas. As a fraternity boy, he endured lost night, the fatuous initiation ceremonies, and the sundry humiliations of pledging. His association with the student newspaper, *The Daily Texan*, opened a window of escape. His first assignment was a weekly column surveying what was being reported by college publications around the country. Here he encountered strange ideas like racial integration, academic freedom, and the possibility that Ike might be something of a bore. Such topics were the exceptions, as most student papers were more concerned with turning over a new leaf at the beginning of each semester, giving blood to the blood drive, collecting wood for the pep rally bonfire, or the virtue of using leisure time more wisely. "Something was out of order here," Willie observed, but the exact nature of his discomfort eluded him (Morris, 162–63).

During this early period at Austin, Morris was invited to the apartment of a young graduate student and his wife. Morris was in awe of the books that lined their walls. Were they some special exhibit? Reflecting on the experience,

Morris writes that it is disconcerting for many southern young people to see great quantities of books in a private home and to listen to ideas seriously discussed away from school. They were talking about ideas for pleasure! When the wife of the graduate student asked him what he wanted to do after graduation, Morris answered that he hoped to become a writer. Surprised by his response, Willie wondered why he had chosen that answer rather than sports announcer—his first vocational choice. That night, fascinated by the discussion and all the books, Morris went to the library determined to read every important book ever written (Morris, 163–64).

Something had happened. Such exposures were beginning to provide Morris "an interest and a curiosity in something outside his own parochial ego." He was beginning to attend not only to the power of language, but also to the exotic world of experience and evocation made accessible by language. Books and literature did not exist for simple casual pleasure but were as "subversive as Socrates and expressions of man's soul." One "dangerous idea" led to another, as Willie's provincial Yazoo mindset succumbed to the subversion of ideas (Morris, 165). Willie's journalism began to focus on such precarious issues as the oil industry's control of the academic life of the University of Texas, the racism of the student body, and the spiritual vacuum of the university community (Morris 169–171).

Just as he was immersing himself in the controversial issues of the early 1950s, Morris traveled back to Yazoo for a few days with family and friends. The locals were buzzing with conversations about a meeting to form local chapter of the White Citizen's Council. The chapter was a response to an NAACP targeting of Yazoo as a location where the Supreme Court desegregation decision would be put in effect. When Morris arrived at the meeting, it was apparent that most of the White citizens of the town were in attendance. He knew them all. Amid cries of "let's get them niggers," the council delegated a list of steps that would be taken. Local Blacks who had signed an NAACP desegregation petition would be immediately evicted by their landlords, barred from buying supplies from White grocers, and fired from their jobs. Morris watched the proceedings with visceral revulsion (Morris, 176–179). He was confronted with the realization that he was not the same person who had lived all his previous life here.

> I looked back and saw my father, sitting still and gazing straight ahead; on the stage my friends' fathers nodded their heads and talked among themselves. I felt an urge to get out of there. *Who are these people?* I asked myself. What was I doing there? Was this the place I had grown up in and never wanted to leave? I knew in that instant, in the middle of a mob in our school auditorium, that a mere three years in Texas had taken me irrevocably, even without me realizing it, from home.[12]

The existential separation of Morris and Yazoo was thus effected. Liberated from unexamined delta consciousness, Morris, like a child taking his first steps, entered gingerly the ranks of that strange group known as southern intellectuals. Southern intellectuals, Morris writes, always had the sense that they were the lucky ones, miraculously freed from all the disastrous alternatives of their isolated lower or middle class rearings. So different was the experience of the eastern Jewish intellectuals who struggled to determine which set of ideas they would accept. For southern intellectuals ideas were not a part of childhood or adolescence, and their discovery in early adulthood as entities worth living by was not taken lightly. We discovered not *certain* books, Morris reflects, "but the simple *presence* of books, not the nuances of idea and feeling, but idea and feeling on their own terms." Because of such a late blooming, southern intellectuals are always cursed and blessed with a hungry, naive quality that eclipses some insights but unveils others.

The southern intellectual is always a man or woman in danger. The exiled Southerner in search of liberation is ever vulnerable to the temptation to turn one's back on his or her own past in the pursuit of some convenient or trendy sophistication. He or she must be aware of the seduction that move one to be dishonest with the most distinctive things about one's self (Morris, 318–19). The attempts of outsiders to dictate what a Southerner *ought* to feel about the South must be resisted. Morris was always impressed with Ellison and Murray's refusal to view their own southern pasts as unmitigated disasters despite the prevailing consensus that they should do so (Morris, 385–86). Since his awakening at the University of Texas, Morris had been ashamed of his Mississippi origins. While in New York, he came to realize that he must transcend such a sentiment, for shame was a simplistic and debilitating emotion, "too easy and predictable—like bitterness." The challenge was to *understand* the southern experience, to comprehend its distinctiveness and meaning in relation to the experiences of humans who came from other places (Morris, 386).

Another threat to Southerners in search of liberation (and to all Southerners for that matter) comes from the rationality of the twentieth century with its industrialization and alienation—the advent of the New South movement. The city of my birth, Jackson, Mississippi, Morris writes, has endured two distinct destructions. The first was engineered with surgeon-like precision by General Sherman in 1863; the second, by ostensibly friendlier hands, came at the urging of the New South developers and entrepreneurs of recent years. These deceivers wrapped themselves in the magical banner of progress while they laid waste the old neighborhoods and city blocks. Rising in the dust were the soulless shopping malls and suburbias—tombstones to much of that sense of continuity, that awareness of human history (Morris 1981).

Of course, the South by any human measure had to reform, but the reform was effected via homogenization. Like in other regions of twentieth century, industrialized America, community in the South began to fade, the ties that bound us together began to disintegrate. There is a painful, twisted ambiguity to the New South of the malls and suburbs. To conquer its racism, sexism, and blood, does the South have to trade in its sense of community for the rampant

commercialism that the Europeans call "Americanization?"
(Morris 1981, 239). The question is omnipresent as Morris
stares at a picture of William Faulkner next to a portrait of
Ronald McDonald in the new McDonald's near the Ole Miss
campus. We cannot avoid the question when we listen to a
member of the Greenwood, Mississippi Chamber of Commerce ask Willie, "What can we do to improve Mississippi's
image?" Let the people of the Bronx or Boston worry about
Mississippi's image, Morris replied, let Mississippians "concern themselves with their image among one another" (Morris, 243). When the material can coerce the human spirit, he
laments, we are doomed (Morris 1967).

The question inevitably arises: Has the South died and
been reincarnated as the Sunbelt? Have the chances for
emancipation bred in pain and suffering already been lost in
a media-soaked postmodern nihilism? Walker Percy sardon-
ically teases radical hopes with his portrayal of Blacks in his
novels. Black Southerners are, as always, estranged in Percy's South, but this time their estrangement is not the result
of the traditional prejudice and oppression; it finds its genesis in alienation, the anomie of late capitalism. Like their
enslavers, they are spiritually alienated, separated from the
world and themselves. Thus, Black progress toward economic
equality, from Percy's perspective, is similar to the South's
quest for mobility—achieved only at a high psychic cost. The
southern Blacks who "make it" economically contract
through their exposure to the alienated marketplace and its
accompanying values the displacement disease. What a
strange form of racial equality Percy proposes—Blacks and
Whites united in their disconnection form history, a postmodern racial rapprochement (Percy 1971; Percy 1977).

The Southerner who seeks authenticity must be aware
of modern industrial alienation, the nature of its southern
manifestation, and its effect on the soul of the individual.
The instrumental rationality that accompanies this alienation precipitates a dishonesty with the most distinctive
things about one's self; indeed, this destruction of self-
knowledge may be its most insidious aspect. We are so physically mutilated by this alienation that we hold in disdain
those who force introspection by inducing us to look beyond

our prevailing common sense view of ourselves so that we might glimpse our essences. While I was in high school, Willie reflects, "I joined easily and thoughtlessly in the Mississippi middle-class consensus that Faulkner, the chronicler and moralist, was out for the Yankee dollar" (Morris 1967, 142). Without an understanding of self, Morris could not possibly understand how he would hold on to and reinterpret that "Mississippi" that would be forever in his soul. Without self-understanding, however, he could not see the connections between himself and Mississippi; he had to transcend it to find it. He had to transcend it to find himself. The southern curriculum must confront the sources of the modern alienation by using its social psychoanalytical methodology. The etiology of the industrial and self-alienation of the sons and daughters of the "good ole boys" and their wives, "the little ladies" must be exposed. The literature on the subject is extensive.

The Treasures

The "southern treasures" that all of us native sons and daughters to some degree hold within us are powerful virtues—virtues not to be romanticized but to be interrogated in their dialectical relationship with the ghosts.

The South is a place where people maintain a closeness to the land and a feel for the rhythms of nature.

The powerful delta land, Willie writes, with all of its mysteries and strengths was always tugging at his soul. During one of his drives through the Mississippi countryside, Willie came upon a Black family in the September fields, burlap sacks of yesteryear draped over their shoulders, picking cotton. As he watched their silhouettes against a darkening sky, he was reminded in that instant of who he was, and where his people came from (Morris 1983). We were never far away from the land, the growing plants, and nature's wilder moods, he tells us. Like the southern past, there was nothing gentle about nature: "It came at you violently, or in a rush, by turns disordered and oppressively somnolent." The overflowing Yazoo River and the tornadoes were especially hard on the poor Blacks, destroying their shacks on stilts built in the river bottoms (Morris 1967). One's closeness to the textures of the land with its sensual if not erotic rhythms staved off at least one form of alienation, as it constantly confronted one with births and deaths, the long forgotten victories and tragedies, and the sadnesses and joys of human existence in this unique place (Morris 1981).

The South is a place where people cherish the importance of friendships that exist in reality, not in the effort—as in a Dale Carnegie "relationship."

Morris is dismayed by the appearance of books in the 1980s on how to cultivate friendships. Such books could only appear in an alienated society where community is crumbling. Friends, in the southern sense of the term, were people one saw frequently and informally, and the word, friendship, carried with it a reverence: "I rank the betrayal of a friend—even a friend from an earlier part of one's life— as dastardly almost as child-abuse or manslaughter" (Morris, 188). In the South, you could organize a party on the spur of the moment and have trouble getting everyone to leave.

You shared certain things: a reverence for informality, an interest in what other friends were doing, a regard for geographic places, an awareness of a certain set of beloved landmarks in themselves important to one's everyday existence, a mutual but usually unexpressed sense of community (Morris 1967, 408). When in New York, Morris, with his southern sensibilities was particularly attentive to the concept of friendship. One could designate a person a "friend," he observed, if "you saw him once every four or five months, talked for a while, and got along." It was absolutely not appropriate to drop in on one's "friends" without warning. "We lunch twice a year," a New Yorker told Willie of a good friend of his. He reported this to me, Willie confides, "without a trace of irony (Morris 1967, 409).

The South is a place where people appreciate the aesthetic of sport while lamenting the questionable values and aggrandizements that threaten its integrity in modern America.

Only with the knowledge that sports was a nexus for what was meaningful to Southerners (Morris 1983a), can we possibly understand that when Willie last spoke with his father as he lay dying of cancer, the subject was baseball. The conversation was by no means trivial; it was very loving and intensely personal (Morris 1967). So were his late night conversations with his grandmother, as they sat together on the front porch of her home discussing the subtleties of the Jackson Senators baseball game and eating her fried chicken that had been soaked overnight in buttermilk (Morris 1981).

The significance of the rituals of sport for Southerners never ceases to impress Willie, who has devoted two of his books about the southern experience to sport. In *The Courting of Marcus Dupree,* Morris uses a Black running back, his high school football career, and the drama of his recruitment to the college ranks as the setting for the story of desegregation in Mississippi. Football illustrates to the Southerner the spectacle of the human adventure and as an observer of the South, Morris contends, he is obliged to watch football not only for its intrinsic aesthetic but also "for the ironic and picturesque detail and for the shadow behind the act" (Morris 1983b). Nothing that mattered so much could fail to reveal something about who we really are. There is a magic to baseball, he writes, a quality that moves the children of the South to a new level of reality ("a dreamy and suspended state") where nothing can penetrate their consciousness while they chase outfield flies (Morris, 103). Sport in the rural South shapes us. Willie recollects the coach of American legion baseball team, a poor farmer known as Gentleman Joe. Before Yazoo's championship game with Greenwood Gentleman Joe delivered his inspirational sermon to the team.

> *Gentlemen,* he said, using that staple designation which earned him his nickname, "I'm just a simple farmer. Fifteen acres is all I got, and two mules, a cow, and a lot of mouths to feed." He paused between his words and his eyes watered over. "I've neglected my little crop because of this

team, and the weevils gave me trouble last year, and
they're doing it again now. I ain't had enough rain, and I
don't plan to get much more. The corn looks so brown, if it
got another shade browner it'd flake right off. But almost
every afternoon you'd find me in my pickup on the way to
town to teach you gentlemen the game of baseball. . . .
Then with his pale blue eyes flashing fire, half whispering
and half shouting, he said: "Gentlemen, I want us to pray,
and then . . . I want you to go out there on that field and
win this Miss'ippi championship. You'll be proud of it for
the rest of your lives. . . . You'll think about it when you're
dyin' and your teeth are all gone."[13]

*The South is a place where people gain a special sensi-
tivity to the struggle of our national experience through the
medium of strained racial relations.*

In the South, Black and White people actually know
each other, and in that knowledge and the knowledge of how
they "knew one another" in the past they gain insight into
the truth and struggle of America's national experience. A
young midwestern journalism professor told Willie that
Black people in Chicago are often strangers to one another,
not to mention to White people (Morris 1983b). In the South,
there is a shared community between White and Black that
hopefully will be strengthened by remembering the past and
by confronting its scars. "I like the way White and Black
people banter with each other," Willie writes, referring to
the racially-conscious kidding that is becoming more and
more common in the South as the wounds start to heal
(Morris 1981). Only those who genuinely understand the
backgrounds of one another can turn the word, "nigger" inside out in order to parody its traditional red-neck usage.
Thus, the word is demystified and the tension engendered
by it diffused. Such a taboo-smashing demystification promotes interracial understanding and unity, not hatred and
divisiveness. During his years in Texas, Willie often debated
where the South ends. At first he thought the boundary was
somewhere a little west of Shreveport but later he came to
realize that it ended where this ambiguous but evolving re-

lationship between Black and White died and one's feel for the guilt of the land faded away (Morris, 77).

The South is a place where people hold the belief that time is a precious entity that an individual controls by not letting it be filled with other-directed and organized activity.

Though the instrumental ethos of the industrialized New South is subverting the effort, Southerners control time better than many. Those long and heavy southern afternoons with nothing doing (Morris 1967), the mystical twilights when one is comforted by the appearance of old friend Venus in the western sky as it oversees the fading of the oranges, violets, mauves, roses, and lavenders below it, the humid evenings when the crickets and frogs provide a musical concert for the patient porch sitter all contribute to an appreciation of the preciousness of time. These are times when one feels best equipped to resist the time thieves with their insidious ability to engender anxiety about the demands of the marketplace. We must never abandon the southern fight to make time stand still without concurrently developing our ability to transcend the blinders of the temporal.

The South is a place where people love storytelling and believe that this tradition builds community by linking us to our past.

In the South, Willie writes, a story worth telling is worth telling again. The storyteller assigns his or her listeners the responsibility to pass the tale along to a different audience, hopefully in a distant future. In this way family and cultural continuity is assured. The stories are the proper province of one's oldest living relative. They are most effective, Morris maintains, when they are told

> in the dark of a summer evening, the whole family gathered on a screened porch, quiet in their listening so that the thumping of the night-flying beetles against the screens and the whine of locusts and cicadas merge with the storyteller's voice to become part of the tale. Such a setting, reaching past into the fiber of childhood, endures as vividly in the memory as the tale itself.[14]

The stories, Willie recalls, detailed the eccentric lives of old ladies of previous generations, recalled the impact of funerals of war heroes and other townspeople, traced tragic love affairs that were never consummated, and painted verbal portraits of old gentlemen with "tobacco stains on their whiskers" (Morris, 239–40). My own southern heritage is exposed by the importance of storytelling in my childhood. The realization that the subjects of my father and mother's stories—their cousins, uncles and aunts (most of whom I never knew)—are more familiar to me in my mind's eye than some of the people I have called *close friends* in my life in the America of the late twentieth century is disconcerting. Eudora Welty extends Morris's reverence for southern storytelling. In the South, status is gained via one's proficiency as a raconteur. One of her characters expresses her desire to marry a particular man for his storytelling ability. Each tale belongs to a larger oral tradition—as Richard Gray puts it:

> a continuum of storytelling: stories knit into one another, one anecdote recalls another in the series, and tales which we learn have been told many times before. . . .[15]

Indeed, the stories help create place and, for that matter, the past.

The South is a place where people revere the impulses of the imagination that shape our speech, our music, our literature, our love of place, and our potential.

The atmosphere of small southern towns, Willie argues, did amazing things to the imagination of its children. When clocks moved slowly the southern sense of fancy had time to develop: "One had to work his imagination out on something" (Morris 1967). Our imagination is our greatest asset; it saved Willie from the philistine concerns of the small town bourgeoisie of Yazoo and it can save the South from the ravages of modern alienation. A student asked Morris if in the face of all the "progress" and "development" Mississippi can retain its spirit:

I told him I did not know. I went on to suggest to the young student, however, that the preservation of those qualities must derive, in the future of Mississippi, from those old impulses of the imagination which have made the literature of Mississippi so impressive. It is no accident, I said, that Mississippi produced Faulkner, and Eudora Welty and Tennessee Williams, and Walker Percy . . . and the distinguished others.[16]

The southern treasures are real and they still breathe despite the standardization of the region. They are found in unlikely places among Black and White, rich and poor, male and female. The obvious caution that must be taken when a writer celebrates such treasures involves the tendency toward romanticization. The innocent country boy (who lives inside me) who played happily and carelessly in the mountains of East Tennessee must not impose his happy images of his South upon my present attempt to garner a mature understanding of the region. The treasures may exist, but they live within a complex dialectic of pain and malformations. Without a critical grounding, the treasures lapse into an apologia for the status quo and the myths that sustain it. Without the treasures, the critical analysis of the South lacks fullness and possibility.

The Possibility of Place

The genre of southern apologia has a long history. At the same time that Willie Morris published *North Toward Home,* Richard Weaver's posthumous defense of the "southern tradition" found its way into print as *The Southern Tradition at Bay.* Weaver's exemplar of the apologia genre highlights the difference between the southern curriculum's guarded celebration of the treasures and a right-wing defense of *Tradition.* To Weaver and his followers the Patriarchal Myth represented the foundation of a southern greatness marked by Christian values, chivalry, men who lived by a gentlemanly code, and the last bastion of honor in

the world. There was little room for gender or racial equal
ity, the deconstruction of social role, socioeconomic mobility,
the values of peace, or social evolution in Weaver's *Tradition.*
Weaver is a self-proclaimed member of the Old Order who
understands that the intrusions of the twentieth century
are destroying the place he loves. It is his identification with
the myths, which grants him the insight needed to understand the changes: "It is not the . . . progressives . . . who
discern what is at issue. . . . It is the men of the old order
who see . . . the implications of the new" (Weaver 1968, 43–
44). The South can continue on its present course to an
amorphous standardized culture, Weaver concludes, or it
can embrace the "fulfillment represented by the Old South"
(Weaver, 391). This is *not* the message conveyed by our exploration of the southern treasures.

Willie Morris senses that buried in the experience of
the South there exists something of great value for America.
The project of the critical analyst of the southern curriculum is to unearth the buried treasures, to chip away the
sediments of racism, sexism, and poverty, and to pursue a
new level of consciousness. The South of the late twentieth
century is a story of people trying—trying to forge a new life
amid the impediments. As usual as the words may sound in
a southern context, I feel that embedded in the southern
treasures is a piece of the *utopian vision* of community—a
vision that may serve as an antidote to the alienation of
modern America. The southern treasures may give us direction in America's coming fight to gain a sense of community
and to repair the ravages of the twentieth century. What
happens in small town Mississippi, Morris contends, will be
of enduring importance to America's quest for its soul (Morris, 123).

Intelligence alone is not enough to fight this twentieth
century alienation. Many of the intellectuals Morris encountered in the Northeast had a empty space where human understanding and toleration should have been. The partisans
of intellectual thrills, Morris observes, seem "to desperately
lack in experiences. . . . They seemed devoid of any serious

concern with real human beings in real human situations"
(Morris 1967). Thus, the southern curriculum based on social psychoanalysis seeks to explore the experiential in relationship to larger social forces. Cora Kaplan writing of
the subordination of women captures the idea when she
calls for an analysis of structures of feelings. Where Kaplan
asks what feelings induce particular women to rebel or sub-
mit, the southern curriculum asks what feelings move a
southern woman to reject the myth of Southern Womanhood
(Kaplan 1986). When confronted with modern southern
alienation such analysis of feeling asks what allows some individuals to sense, expose, and overcome the deleterious effects of alienation in their lives and what blinds others to its
existence.

Henry Giroux writes that one way technical/instrumen-
tal rationality contributes to the alienation of twentieth century life involves the fact that scholarship, theory, and
intellectual pursuit are seen to posses no ethical dimension
(Giroux 1988). Scholarship serves the end of collecting "objective facts" that can be empirically verified. Thus, modern
scholarship of this like has turned its back on the classical
Greek notion that academic activity was designed as a
method to free humans from dogma so that they could pursue ethical action (Giroux 1981). Reflecting on his teacher,
Texas newspaper editor Ronnie Dugger, Morris tells us that
Dugger didn't simply teach him the techniques of reporting
and writing, but how to view public life as an ethical process
(Morris 1967).

I revere the southern treasures; their humanity, authenticity, and ethical orientation make me confront who I
really am and the relationship between that person and who
I would really like to be. The southern personality treasures
offer a stark contrast to the so-called objective view of the
world often taught in our elementary schools, high schools,
and colleges, promoted in our businesses, and ground into
our consciousness by television. The southern sense of history, its collective memory, may yield an American sense of
possibility. Joan Didion writes that a "place belongs forever

to whoever remembers it most obsessively, wrenches it from itself, shapes it, renders it, loves it so radically that he remakes it in his image" (Morris 1981). Our memory, our understanding of the historical forces that pull our puppet strings, can liberate us, and hopefully save us. It is this vision that inspires the southern curriculum.

---

*To "Manny" Pridgen, a southern scholar, who first introduced me to the South as "place. "

6

The New South as Curriculum: Implications for Understanding Southern Race Relations

—————————— *Louis A. Castenell, Jr.*

Southern culture shapes the corpus of knowledge transmitted through the overt and null curricula, thereby influencing race relations. W. H. Schubert (1986) describes the overt curriculum as consisting of all skills, concepts, principles, appreciations, and values that school officials overtly provide for students. Curriculum specialists are aware that within this overt context there exists information, attitudes, values, principles, and concepts that are learned by what is not taught in the schools. E. W. Eisner (1979) refers to this as the null curriculum. For example, the absence of Black achievers in a history text teaches that Blacks did not make major contributions to our society and to the international community in general.

The tragedies of the past are still unresolved. Schools reflect this collective indecisiveness. It is inside the organization of school that education becomes a function of place, place in the sense that lived experiences of people within a region give meaning to their political, economic, social, and religious orientations. Thus, the three questions that will direct this effort are: What is southern culture? Is there a difference between the Old and the New South? Finally, how have interpretations of past events affected school curriculum?

Southern Culture

The factors that shaped a distinctive South are: (*a*) the relative absence of non-Anglo-Saxon White ethnics, (*b*) fundamentalist Protestantism, and (*c*) a propensity for violence manifested in the peculiar racial and economic institution of the slave plantation (Carter 1981). As pressure was applied on the South to abandon slavery, white Southerners began to see themselves as sharing a common culture, sharing the same values and goals. By 1840, southern historians shifted from a history that asserted the various southern states' peculiar contributions to America to a history that asserted the South's difference from the North as spiritually superior (Franklin 1960). Since history was a popular and influential form of literature at that time, southern historians legitimated prevailing social attitudes. Just as important, the South was economically dependent on a plantation economy, one that was based on the exploitation of Blacks and the subjugation of women. Thus, the plantation social system and economy supported existing class, race, and gender relationships.

These relationships were complex and interrelated. One means to maintain social order was authority (Mandle 1978). Authority resulted in laws and regulations governing behavior that provided the plantation a high degree of autonomy and sovereignty according to J. R. Mandale. These laws and regulations made it possible for white Southerners to exploit Blacks by committing acts of violence and intimidation against Black men and women. The class structure was maintained primarily by serving as a symbol for what poor Whites could aspire to. And finally, authority permitted White men the right to deny White women their right to be self-determined and instead placed them on a pedestal.

Southern culture shifted drastically after the Civil War. Though conditions did not change substantially for women and poor Whites until the middle of the twentieth century, Reconstruction and its aftermath radically changed race relations. According to D. H. Donald (1981) many Southerners' old feelings of condescending benevolence toward Blacks was replaced with absolute hatred. This hatred grew as white Southerners were forced to accept a new social order, one that gave Blacks limited but important political and economic opportunities. Because Whites in the South were unwilling to accept changes, they manufactured the idea of a Lost Cause. C. G. Sellers wrote:

> Bitter with defeat and humiliation in the postwar years, Southerners sought emotional balm in the sentimental myth of the Lost Cause, a pseudo-tragedy which gave the South a false history, a false image of itself, and a mystical social ideal that Southerners had not really accepted even in the heyday of secession.[1]

Southern culture became the Lost Cause. Southern writers and scholars celebrated their "heroic" struggle against the invading "Yankees" with pageantries and monuments of battles won and lost. In literature, southern writers began to create psuedo-scientific documents perpetuating Blacks as inherently lazy, sexually deviant, biologically inferior, and a general menace to the community (Frederickson 1971). One of the best selling authors in the early twentieth century was Thomas Dixon. In *The Leopard's Spots,* Dixon described how the Civil War and Reconstruction turned Blacks from:

> chattel to be bought and sold into a possible beast to be feared and guarded. . . . a menace throwing the blight of its shadow over future generations, a veritable Black Death for the land and its people.[2]

In referencing women, southern mythos denied women of both races sexual self-determination (Gwin 1985). K. Fishburn (1982), argued:

> Whereas the lady was deprived of her sexuality, the Black woman was identified with hers. White women were characterzied by their delicate constitutions, sexual purity and

moral superiority to men and Black women were sub-
human creatures who, by nature, were strong and sexual.[3]

Racial animosity simmered until the 1880s when the South
was returned to southern leadership. Cultural contacts were
violent and exploitative. Social etiquette called for a return
to the antebellum system of relations (Mandle 1978).
Schools became the new authoritative institution to teach
prevailing social norms. Because Whites convinced themselves that Blacks were intellectually inferior, separate but
unequal schools were funded. The miseducation of Black and
White youngsters became generational. During this time,
laws were also passed that completely disfranchised Blacks
politically, economically, and socially (Berghe 1967). For the
next eighty-five years the old South reigned.

Old South v. New South

Two major laws that were enacted that eventually gave
birth to the New South and changed southern culture were:
(a) the Civil Rights Act of 1964, and (b) the Voting Rights Act
of 1965. Each of these laws made it possible for Blacks to
reenter mainstream society. These significant pieces of legislation empowered Blacks; they changed past social patterns.
The Lost Cause became largely symbolic. Southern White
leaders, particularly in large urban areas, became accepting
of a new social order, albeit reluctantly. Southern reformers,
Black and White, began to promote change to improve their
respective social and economic opportunities. Thus, the New
South came to be a place marketed as rich in history, economically advantageous for industrial/technological growth,
and free of the racial turmoil that characterized the past.
Though an appealing concept, the question remains, Is the
New South really different from the Old South?
    The New South is fundamentally different from the Old
South in that there is a redistribution of economic and political resources. Educationally, the South leads the country in

school desegregation (King 1979). Nonetheless the legacy of the past can be observed upon closer inspections of recent educational, political, and economic gains of Blacks.

Though the South leads the country in desegregated schools, there still remains serious problems. W. King (1979) reported the hiring of fewer minority teachers has not kept pace with Black enrollments. "In the South, where 34 percent of the elementary and secondary school children are Black, only 24 percent of the teachers are."[4] The continued underfunding of schools attended by Blacks is problematic. In seven states, Blacks represent more than 20 percent of the population (Mississippi (35 percent), South Carolina (34 percent), Louisiana (29 percent), Georgia (27 percent), Alabama (26 percent), Maryland (23 percent), and North Carolina (22 percent). A. M. Garibaldi (1986) concluded:

> All of these states have more than 30 percent minority students in their respective school systems and only one (Maryland) has a per pupil expenditure ranked above 30, placing them among the lowest state in per pupil expenditure when compared with the 50 states and the District of Columbia.[5]

Recently Judge Neal Biggers, a President Reagan appointee, dismissed a lawsuit that charged Mississippi with illegally operating a racially segregated higher education system (Jaschik 1988): Judge Biggers ruled:

> ... the groups that filed the suit had been able to prove that Black and White students enrolled in colleges at different rates and that historically Black and historically White colleges received disparate amounts of state support. But he said such evidence alone did not prove illegal or unconstitutional discrimination.[6]

Black economic gains in the South are significantly improved since 1970 according to A. Karning and P. McClain (1985). They pointed out that as economic conditions increased in the South, skilled and better educated Blacks moved to the South. "Between 1975 and 1980, nearly one-half million Blacks moved South."[7] However, the findings of a T-test analysis concluded that gains achieved by southern Blacks were less substantial than in other regions. For example:

> the median Black income in southern cities is 11,094, whereas it is 14,584 in nonsouthern cities. . . . In 1980, Black median income in southern cities was only 55.8 percent of White median income. . . . In nonsouthern cities, the ratio was 70.9 percent.[8]

Black Southerners have achieved the most politically. According to the Joint Center for Political Studies (Cohen 1988), the number of Black elected officials increased from 1,469 in 1970 to 6,681 in 1987. In that same time, the number of mayors rose from 48 to 303; Congressional members rose from 10 to 23; statewide office holders rose from one to five; State senators rose from 137 to 311; and 64.5 percent of Black elected officials are in the South, where 52.8 percent of American's Black population lives. Though these data speak volumes for Black achievement, there is some reason for caution. J. W. Moore (1981) posited that due to major fiscal problems Black politicians must not only find substitutes for strong local power bases, but also, they usually lack strong bases with local White-controlled corporate powers. The Black political elite is too financially dependent on White elite support for any radical restructuring of governance.

School Curriculum

Southern schools like other schools in the country are dependent on published materials to teach their classes. Curriculum therefore is largely limited to standardized, grade level specific text (Apple 1988). According to M. W. Apple, "75 percent of the time elementary and secondary students are in classrooms and 90 percent of the time they assign to homework is spent with text materials."[9] A careful examination of what is taught in three southern states, (Louisiana, Mississippi, and Virginia) sheds light on how southern culture permeates the curriculum.

Since history is a subject used by states to teach their past, reviewing history texts reveal popular interpretations. D. B. Fleming (1987) studied how slavery, which is treated in high school textbooks, is approved by the state of Virginia. He concluded that variations were considerable, both in the amount of coverage and in specific details. "Of the fourteen books reviewed only three gave little attention to slave life and none gave slave life any form of favorable treatment."[10] However Fleming did point out that copies of earlier books can be found in schools as required texts. These earlier books described slavery as an enjoyable experience for Blacks. "Generally speaking, the slave's food was plentiful, his clothing adequate, his cabin warm, his health protected, his leisure carefree. . . . slaves enjoyed collective social security" (Hamphill et.al. 1957, 120).

Robert Moore (1980) judged the only required history text used in Mississippi schools to be too distorted, biased, and full of omissions. John Bettersworth's text *Your Mississippi* minimized the brutality of slavery limiting the treatment of slaves to four paragraphs. The author makes no mention of segregation or lynching. Though other textbooks can be found in Mississippi, Bettersworth's book is still popular reading.

In Louisiana, two history books are placed in most schools—*Louisiana: The Land and Its People* and *Our Louisiana Legacy*. Both textbooks treat the past in ways that celebrated the Lost Cause. For example, Sue Eaken and M. Culbertson's *Louisiana: The Land and Its People* described relationships on the plantation as happy. "Natural ties of affection developed among many of these people who were dependent upon one another as owners and slaves."[11] The authors further stated that most slaves enjoyed regular rest days and vacations.[12](p.275). In H. Dethloff and A. Begnaud's *Our Louisiana Legacy* slaves were "sufficiently fed, clothed and housed. . . . Although the treatment of slaves may not have been overly harsh, the fact that one was not free must have been a terrible burden."[13]

These writers conveniently avoided the horrors of slavery to appease the white Southerners' sensibility and to make a buck. On one hand, in not addressing the social, political, educational, and economic ramifications of slavery and segregation *de jure*, southern writers have by omission heightened racial tensions and misunderstandings. Blacks resent the mollification of their history and experiences and perceive southern nostalgia as overt racism. Concomitantly, Whites choose to recall selective aspects of southern history in order to avoid a reconciliation of their tumultuous and tragic past. Consequentially, the null curriculum condemns Whites to provincial attitudes and outlooks consistent with racial hegemony. On the other hand, books that are not profitable are not viewed favorably by publishers (Apple 1988). Thus, southern culture as the Lost Cause continues to be manufactured due to the financial power of the White elite. In this way the overt curriculum and null curriculum perpetuate southern mythology.

Conclusion

We have seen how the struggles between Blacks and Whites in the southern states gave meaning to southern culture. Today scholars of the American South are redefining southern culture to incorporate the experiences of Blacks and members of ethnic groups (Winkler 1988). No longer in learned communities is southern culture considered only White. "Because Black people have played such a significant role in Southern history, the redefinition of southern culture focuses particularly on reclaiming their experience."[14]

The New South's glory days are gone (Katz 1988). From the early 1970s to the mid-1980s, the era brought prosperity to much of the region, however industry has begun relocation to Third World countries (C–2). Presently, the future of the New South is uncertain. Nonetheless, southern leaders view an improved educational system as a step in the right direction.

For significant social change to occur, Black and White students need a new curriculum, a curriculum free of distortions, myths, and legends. These students should be challenged to face the future for "those whose pride in past and present renders them identical with what they have been conditioned to be, and thus profoundly ignorant of what they might strive to become."[15]

7

Curriculum as Social Psychoanalysis: On the Significance of Place

William F. Pinar

Place as a concept is largely absent in the curriculum literature, predictably so. From its conception as a specialized field this century, curriculum has tended toward the abstract, for instance the formulation of principles of curriculum development applicable anytime and anywhere. In contrast, one strand of contemporary curriculum discourse (Miller 1988) exemplifies an autobiographically situated portrait of curriculum experience. Another exemplifies historically and politically situated understandings of curriculum issues (Whitson in Pinar 1988). In the present study, curriculum will be situated geographically, that is, in the "South," and a program of study that is appropriate to this American region at this historical conjuncture will be briefly outlined. Such a curriculum not only represents a "place," but it also becomes "place," a curricular embodiment and contradiction of peculiarly southern experience, taught in ways appropriate to that experience, toward the end of demystifying southern history. As "place" or "ground" in Gestalt terms, this curriculum as a form of social psychoanalysis permits the student to emerge as figure, capable of critical participation in a historical present hitherto denied. I contend that the educational and economic development of the region requires both.

Place

The trend toward curriculum standardization mirrors the macro-trend toward cultural homogenization. As educational historians have described, this curricular trend developed as a response to the mass entry of immigrants to the United States during the period 1890–1930. As well, the continuing evolution of an industrial civilization toward an increasingly corporatized one required increasing mobility, especially in the managerial classes. As one commentator on the importance of "place" and locale in southern experience has noted, a nomadic people tends to deemphasize place as significant (Dabbs 1964). There are those who argue that regional or sectional differences are inconsequential, given the rise of the New South, (clearly a South newer in, say, Virginia and North Carolina than in Louisiana and Mississippi). Actually, the notion of a New South is a century old (Genovese 1968), and while referring to actual demographic, economic, and cultural shifts, the concept also functions to obscure and even deny the considerable extent to which the specific history of this region echoes in the lives of its present inhabitants. This denial is psychological, as students of the South as varied As W. J. Cash and Lewis Simpson have described. To bring this denial to individual and collective awareness is, in my view, a timely curricular priority, as the consequences of this denial include distortions in several spheres. These include, but are not limited to, the domains of race, class, and gender. My intention here is to review these "echoes" or spheres and suggest a curriculum that might function to both articulate and surpass them.

Every region has its history, of course. Why might studying the history of the South for Southerners be more important than studying the history of, say, the Midwest for midwesterners? The reasons are two, I believe. One involves the southern history of slavery, war, defeat, and relative poverty. As literary historian, Lewis Simpson has noted, Southerners have responded to this legacy by "forgetting" it. In Simpson's terms, both history and memory were lost in the aftermath of the Civil War and Reconstruction. Journalist and student of the "mind of the South" W. J. Cash asserts that Southerners have retreated from the facts of their history to fictions and fantasies. This phenomenon of denial and flight from reality involves, unsurprisingly, distortions in several spheres, distortions that undermine the South's efforts to develop economically and culturally. For such development to occur, the South must avoid efforts to merely "Northernize" it (Clement 1983). Rather, it must experience cultural renewal on its own terms (terms which do involve the North, of course). Renewal, however, for those estranged from their own histories, requires a social psychoanalytic process the curricular elements of which I will suggest later. Suffice to say now that the South differs from the Midwest, the West, or New England in its particular history and perhaps more importantly, in its response to that history. Second, the power of place as a category of social and personal experience is strong in the South. Students of the South from various disciplines testify to the power of "place" in southern political and literary history. As historian David Potter observes:

> It was an aspect of this culture that the relation between land and people remained more direct and more primal in the South than in other parts of the country. (This may be more true for the Negroes than for the Whites, but then there is also a question whether the Negroes have not embodied the distinctive qualities of the Southern character even more than the Whites.)[1]

An intensified relation to place and a psychological denial of the facts of the southern experience suggest the appropriateness of attention to southern history. As Potter's remark implies, this history, this place, is a fundamentally African-American place.

Race

In contrast to the sentimentalized view of American slavery expressed in popular fiction like Margaret Mitchell's *Gone with the Wind*, slave historians debate just how bestial the system was, on its own terms and compared to other systems of slavery. Stanley Elkins' controversial study suggests that the racial stereotype of "Sambo," ignorant, innocent, and loyal, has a basis in the actual experience of slavery. Using Sullivan's psychosocial theory of "significant others", Elkins reconstructs a process of mass infantilization, a process of destruction of the slaves' personalities. In Elkins' view, the child-like Sambo represented the mutilated fragment of human personality remaining after the slave system crushed the kidnapped Africans. Elkins' compares the slave system, and the Sambo result, to the Nazi extermination camps of World War II (Elkins 1959).

While not dissenting from the general view of slavery as bestial, other students of slavery see a more complicated picture. For instance, Eugene Genovese criticizes the "onesidedness" of Elkins' study, characterizing it as deterministic. In reducing all aspects of slave life to the mass infantilization model and the concentration camp parallel, Elkins ignores the slaves' struggles to undermine the slaveholders' authority, as well as the slaves' creation of culturally self-affirmative rituals and behaviors. Genovese views slaves and slaveholders as culturally and politically intertwined. So understood, the concept of "South" is a fundamentally Black as well as White concept (Genovese 1968). Also depicting the slaves' capacity for rebellion, Gilmore contests the conventional view of Christianity as politically emasculating. Instead, Gilmore suggests, Christianity played a central role in slave rebellion. He traces recent expressions of African-American radicalism to these rebellions (Wilmore 1983).

The extent to which slavery was a moral issue in the political crisis, which became the Civil War (or the Southern War for Independence, as more than one southern writer has characterized it), has been debated extensively in the literature. Not surprisingly, southern historians tend to view the issue as primarily political, involving in a central way the issue of "states rights" (Cooper 1978). While the moral issue was paramount for the abolitionists, there is evidence to suggest that Lincoln and others used the slavery issue as a political lever. Further, it is clear that the North profitted indirectly from slave labor (Genovese 1968). Further undermining the view of the North as morally superior in this conflict is the experience of those escaped slaves who joined the northern army. These soldiers faced humiliating racial prejudice, despite which, by all accounts, they performed bravely. The deposit remaining today in mass culture is a lingering sense of moral superiority and self-righteousness in the North. As African-American experience in the North suggests, this sense of moral superiority is not warranted. In the South remains a defensiveness regarding race, including a denial of guilt and responsibility for enslavement and consequent segregation, prejudice, and violence. As the Genovese thesis of inseparability implies, southern Whites and African-Americans probably must re-experience their past intimacy, however politically vertical its past structure was, and renegotiate its terms. Until that process is undertaken and accomplished, distortions in both personalities will linger, a persisting sense of defeat in southern Blacks and a sense of false superiority in southern Whites. These issues, while racially born, become in the present era, more dominantly class issues.

Class

The myth of a southern aristocracy is as strong as it is false. As W. J. Cash and others have pointed out, a true aristocracy does not choose to travel an immense ocean and settle a primitive frontier (Cash 1941). Those who came to the South sought economic opportunity and escape. The immigrants' creation of slavery and plantation life was hardly an extension of a genteel life lived in Europe. The early plantation owners, relatively few in number, were "rough and ready types" whose capacity for alcohol consumption and violence was highly developed. Many more Whites were "yeoman," small landowners with fewer than five slaves or with no slaves at all. The profound class difference between these two groups was obscured by the presence of slaves who provided a permanent class "floor" to southern White society. As well, the personalism of an agrarian culture in which many inhabitants of a particular county or parish were indeed members of the same extended family, numbed working and poor Whites to the sharp social and economic inequities the political economy of slavery guaranteed. Within slavery, house slaves tended to assume superior class positions to those who worked the land. Some evidence suggests the former class formed the beginnings of the African-American bourgeoisie (Genovese 1964).

While African-Americans remain the underclass in the South today, some upward mobility is visible. (Political power appears to be on the increase, note the political power accumulated in Atlanta and political victories for Reverend Jesse Jackson in several southern states in the Democratic Party presidential primaries on so-called Super Tuesday 1988.) Despite change, still noticeably absent in the South are the assertiveness and willingness to contest racism observable among some African-American citizens living in the North. Southern African-Americans *know* that southern Whites fought and died to keep them enslaved, then devised systems of segregation and fought violently to retain them. Northern African-Americans know that the non-racist claims of Northern Whites are often just pretense, and understandably respond to them with indignation. In both instances, White antagonism is related not only to racism but also to perceived economic competition, increased by federal antidiscrimination legislation and periodic contraction in the manufacturing and industrial sectors. In the South, the issue is decidedly class, intertwined as it is with race. Condemmed by many Whites to a permanent underclass status due to race, African-Americans' economic and cultural emergence undermines the White-defined class structure of the South. Poor Whites have allowed their racial prejudice to keep them complacent. No matter how poor and how failed Whites are, their view is that there remains a class underneath them. William Faulkner portrays in powerful ways the self-destructiveness of the southern racial and class system for poor and working Whites, as well as for African-Americans (Faulkner 1946).

Gender

In behavior and in musculture, men and women exhibit more masculinized and feminized characteristics respectively, than do many in the North. Stylized versions of masculinity and femininity, while hardly restricted to the South, did accompany the slave system and plantation life. The myth of the (White) southern woman can be traced to these developments—highly feminized, vulnerable yet resourceful, always the lady—as can the myth of the (White) southern man—masculine, invulnerable, masterful, always the gentleman. The plantation owner so mytholgized "his lady" (the myth of purity implies sexual inaccessibility) that he turned regularly to African-American slave women to satisfy his often violent desire. His fear that many African-American men schemed to rape White women may represent a fantasy, in which the former's sexual prowess is threatening to the masculinity of the latter. There could be a latent homoeroticism here which, because it is denied, gets projected onto the woman. As psychoanalysis knows, fear is often inverted desire.

If gender polarizations are associated with specific historical periods and forms of production (Pinar n.d.), then the South's agrarian past and present, the relative recentness of industrialization and corporatization, make intelligible contemporary gender patterns in the South. While relatively hypermasculinized and feminized, they are mediated by the mass culture industry, wherein some sexual ambiguity and somewhat altered gender relations are regularly presented. Thus, the present situation, while overtly layered with antiquated gender forms, is approaching fluidity and indeed instability. Articulations of gender, and in particular articulations of the status of women in the South, become more urgent, while institutional support for such work, say in women's studies programs, remains inadequate. This inadequacy of response originates in ignorance of gender, that is, in its taken-for-grantedness, and in willful efforts to conserve past gender arrangements. As well, it resides in the particular ways that gender and family configurations in the South functioned to resist institutionalization generally (Genovese 1968). To this issue we turn next.

Private Space and the Public Domain

It is non-controversial, I believe, to observe that the concept of public domain remains underdeveloped in the South, with attendant underdevelopment of the constituent institutional forms of that domain, including education. Let us review two related elements: gender and family.

The plantation system was precapitalistic (although it participated in capitalism) and pre-bourgeois in class structure. The social structure of three centuries of slavery are summarized by Gilberto Freyre: "The power of the great planters was indeed feudalistic, their patriarchalism being hardly restricted by civil laws" (Freyre 1963). The plantation owners owned all: wives, children, and slaves. They established the laws of life, and in so doing usurped the role of public institutions, including legal ones. Law and its enforcement remained particularized and embodied in the person of the landowner, extending feudal social organization well into the nineteenth century. The articulation of "states rights" in the southern rationale for secession can be understood as a political expression of patriarchy and its projection into the public sphere (Phillips 1963). Indeed, the public sphere was viewed as an extension of private space.

After the destruction of plantation life in the Civil War, Whites recoiled from a public sphere suddenly controlled by African-Americans and Northerners. The concept of public school, antebellum in origin but introduced on a mass scale during Reconstruction, was viewed as anatagonistic to southern social organization and to "the southern way of life." That way of life conceived the public sphere as an extension of the private one. No longer controlling the public domain, Whites did more than withdraw from it; they both passively and actively resisted its development.

This resistance was aggravated by the Civil Rights movement and federally mandated desegregation of public places. Predictably, investment in the public domain has been and remains minimal. (This fact varies of course; public investment is greater, say, in Virginia than in, say, Louisiana.) Indeed public monies are sometimes viewed as opportunities for private gain, as the corrupt political history of Louisiana, for instance, indicates. All forms of institutional life, from educational to the legal, remain underdeveloped today in the South. To reclaim the public space will require reclaiming the history of its disclaiming. No simple memorization of the facts of southern history will permit the psychological and intellectual "working through" that is necessary now. A social psychoanalytic curriculum of interdisciplinary southern studies might.

Curriculum as Social Psychoanalysis

There is no such thing really as was, because the past is.

William Faulkner

Presentism is hardly peculiar to the South. Historians have lamented its persistence as a central feature of contemporary American life; it has been intensified in an imagistic culture associated with mass advertising and the culture industry, and in the presence of "radical evil." For Christopher Lasch this radical evil is Nazi Germany and the extermination of Jews, a historical fact, he argues, unassimilable by a rational mass consciousness. The unassimilability and unintelligibility of racial extermination coupled with an unstable public sphere partially created by the culture industry and threatened by nuclear war, results in a presentistic and solipsistic self (Lasch 1984). The curricular task becomes to recover memory and history in ways that psychologically allow individuals to reenter politically the public sphere in meaningful and committed ways.

Presentism accompanies public school curricula in the South. Here the distinction between school knowledge and authentic academic knowledge is perhaps even more pronounced than it is in other regions of the country. There seems to be even more mistaking of busy-work for learning, more mistaking bureaucratic authority for intellectual authority. In the South even more than in the North, curriculum becomes an anonymous Other whose linkages to everyday life are fragile and implicit. In other terms, Apollonian and Dionysian impulses are profoundly alienated from each another, a schizoid state of affairs evident in Louisiana, for instance, where Mardi Gras and radical Christian fundamentalism (such as that of Jimmy Swaggert, based in Baton Rouge) coexist. The curriculum tends to function in the South not unlike a secular version of biblical fundamentalism, in which the letter of text is mistaken for its spirit. In both versions of what we might loosely term positivism, the South's distance from the centers of knowledge production recall its defeated and victimized status, its position of "recipient" of the Word. Patriarchal loyalty to the Other requires a strict, literal rendering of the text, stunting both intellectual and spiritual development. Hedonism, split off from rational articulation and integration with daily life, threatens to become all-consuming for those whose pleasure-seeking lacks rational restraint. The pleasure of the text, to use Barthes' felicitous phrase linking sensuality and knowledge, is in principle difficult to experience in the South.

These "split-offs" are maintained by a presentism that assumes that a past forgotten is a past no longer present. As psychoanalysis has demonstrated and southern novelists like Faulkner have portrayed, the past remains. Given the South's particular history, and given its sharp sense of "place," the past figures prominently in the southern present, despite protestations to the contrary. Even should southern schools adopt the most technically accurate and refined curriculum, until the South reexperiences its past in ways that allow it, in Lewis Simpson's phrase, to recover memory and history, southern students will not fully learn it. Culturally and psychosocially dysfunctional patterns will continue. What I wish to propose here is a curriculum of place, a ground for the technical curricula (the sciences, for instance) being emphasized today. This is a curriculum of southern studies whose objective is not a sentimentalization of the past, or a sectional version of nationalism, but rather a psychoanalytically informed interdisciplinary study and reexperience of the past, so that White guilt can be acknowledged, responsibility can be claimed, and perhaps forgiven as African-Americans rediscover to an extent perhaps they have not yet their strengths, courage, and competence. Unless this process occurs culturally and individually, the South will probably continue to live out—perhaps unconsciously—its history of relative poverty, defeat, racism, and class privilege.

Curriculum as Place

As Lewis Simpson observes in his classic *The Dispossessed Garden,* the South lost both history and memory in defending its agrarian way of life, in its denial of its status as, in Simpson's phrase, the "garden of chattel." The southern literary Renaissance of the early twentieth century, most prominently associated with the names of William Faulkner, Robert Penn Warren, Eudora Welty, Thomas Wolfe, and others, involved the recovery of both history and memory. The presence of the past in the present is portrayed, for instance, in this remarkable passage from William Faulkner's *Intruder in the Dust.* It suggests the meaning of the Battle of Gettysburg for the southern consciousness.

> It's all now see. Yesterday wont be over until tomorrow and tomorrow began ten thousand years ago. For every Southern boy fourteen years old, not once but whenever he wants it, there is the instant when it's still not yet two

o'clock on that July afternoon in 1863, the brigades are in
position behind the rail fence, the guns are laid and ready
in the woods, and the furled flags are already loosened to
break out, and Pickett himself with his long oiled ringlets
and his hat in one hand probably and his sword in the
other looking up the hill waiting for Longstreet to give the
word and it's all in the balance, it hasn't happened yet, it
hasn't even begun yet, it not only hasn't begun yet but
there is still time for it not to begin against that position
and those circumstances which made more men that Gar-
nett and Kemper and Armstead [*sic*] and Wilcox look grave
yet it's going to begin, we all know that, we have come too
far with too much at stake and that moment doesn't need
even a fourteen-year-old boy to think This time. Maybe
this time with all this much to lose and all this much to
gain; Pennsylvania, Maryland, the world, the golden dome
of Washington itself to crown with desperate and unbeliev-
able victory the gamble, the case made two years ago; or to
anyone who ever sailed even a skiff under a quilt sail, the
moment in 1492 when somebody thought This is it; the absolute edge of no return, to turn back now and make home
or sail irrevocably on and either find land or plunge over
the world's roaring rim.[2]

What has been achieved in the southern literary imagination remains only partially achieved in southern
mass culture. Recent economic gains, reversing slowly the
century-old economic underdevelopment of the region, coupled with a cultural "imperialism" of the mass media (southern voices continue to disappear from television and radio
for example), support Southerners in their repression of history, a history that differs painfully from that of the North.
This pain is comprised by, in addition to its contrasting economic history, its absence of that moral self-righteousness
associated with New England Puritanism, accompanied as
that is by a sense of invincibility, optimism, and guilt. It is
painful for (White) Southerners to remember that the South
lost the only war it waged. The pain repressed produces pes-
simism, which in its turn supports nostaligia, which in turn
supports provincialism, conservatism, and the racial class

system. The democratic legacy of the New England town meeting is missing in the plantation South with its acute, if denied, system of racial caste. (Woodward 1968).

The repression of memory and history is accompanied by distortions of various kinds, including political, social, racial, and psychological distortions. These distortions function to undermine the South's efforts to develop the intelligence and economic competitiveness of its citizens. Thus, the greatest incentive for the South today to unearth its past is not the intrinsic worth of the project, although it is intrinsically worthwhile. The incentive today would be to create that individual and social awareness that is a fundamental concomitant to the development of intelligence in its various modes, including technical, psychosocial, and aesthetic intelligence (Gardner 1983). The South cannot easily compete economically with other regions of the country, particularly the Northeast and West Coast, until in psychoanalytic fashion it reexperiences its past in ways that will free the present from the past. To put the matter another way, the contemporary task of economic renewal requires a simultaneous cultural renewal, a curricular provocation of which might be southern studies. These programs must not function as pretexts for nostalgia. The curriculum would be comprised of politically critical and informed analyses of the "world the slaveholders made." Genovese's various studies of slavery and of African-American history generally represent one such a perspective, a perspective that would be supplemented by not only conservative historians, but by African-American historians and writers, including but hardly limited to Maya Angelou, James Baldwin, William Edward DuBois, Alice Walker, Robert Wright. A central theme of these southern studies would be the multiracial character of the South, the profound ways in which African-American and Whites are two ethnic sides of the same cultural coin. Only when southern Whites comprehend that their experience is inseparable from that of southern African-Americans (and vice versa) can the history of each group, merged and denied as it is, be reexperienced, psychologically accepted, and its genocidal aspects perhaps forgiven and surpassed.

Obviously, this is an enormous pedagogical and cultural task. However, the size and complexity of the task cannot be permitted to function as a rationalization not to attempt it. The educational development of the South, in a post-industrial period (just dawning in the South) when economic and cultural development are intertwined, depends upon it. Second, the history of class, racially and within White and African-American sectors, must be made explicit, understood and "lived through." As we know, the presence of slaves blurred class distinctions between the small aristocracy and the larger working and poor White classes, with the effect of blinding the White working class and poor Whites to their true status, undermining their efforts to economically and culturally further themselves. Indeed, poor and lower middle-class Whites continue to misunderstand their status vis-á-vis the White upper class, and displace their frustration onto each other and onto African-Americans. Racism is the key issue here, and thus it is listed first in this curricular rationale for southern studies. Due to its intimacy with race, class is listed second. The aforementioned class issues can be delineated and taught in an intergrated study of the literature, history, economics, and sociology of the South. A history and analysis of class relations within the African-American sector are essential. Third, a history of gender is required to comprehend the particular ways that women, both White and African-American, were conceptualized and socially placed (Fox-Genovese 1988). The often heroic history of African-American women, as they supported slave families in which African-American men were marginalized by White slaveowners, needs to be taught and psychologically incorporated. The possible latent homoeroticism between the White slaveholders and their African-American male slaves, transfigured into a fear of African-American desire for White women (the White women in them, in Jungian terms) needs to be articulated. (Eldridge Cleaver, in his brilliant if polemic *Soul On Ice*, comprehends, if from a heterosexist perspective, this dynamic.) The passive aggression of slaveholders toward their wives and daughters as they mystified them into objects of hyper-femininity and social uselessness needs to be theorized and taught. Also to be taught would be the sophisticated responses of these women, including their strategies of self-affirmation and empowerment, as well their displacement of frustration onto each other and upon their racial captives. Fourth, the struggle and triumph of African-American men, as they often appeared to comply with their masters but retained and sometimes strengthened an autonomous and undefeated psychological and cultural core—which led a hundred years later to African-American nationalism and separatism—needs to detailed. Each of these thematizations needs to be studied and reexperienced and integrated in the present (Genovese 1968). Finally, the configuration of elements involved in the South/North relationship needs to be examined and experienced, including what Clement terms "northernizing the south" (Clement 1983). Those of us who have been born and who have lived in the North but who live now in the South must participate in this examination, as our memory of and history with the South, while perhaps not repressed, is deformed. What is deformed includes our insistence upon the exclusively moral character of the Civil War, contributing to our self-righteousness at our perceived moral superiority, our pretentions regarding the absence of racism in the North, and our assumed cultural (including linguistic) sophistication and superiority. All of this gets mixed up with a regional version of racism, of course, and this, too, must be confronted directly.

While history and literature would constitute the two major disciplines comprising this conception of southern studies, the other disciplines comprising the humanities, the arts, and the social sciences obviously have curricular roles to play. Given the racial and gender tendencies of these fields, departments of Black and Women's studies need to be involved in central ways. True, courses in southern history and literature have been offered for decades. However, a review of university catalogues reveals—while extant (see appendix)—that programs in southern studies are uncommon. (Offerings in the lower schools are less common still). My contention is that the social psychoanalytic potential of crit-

ically informed southern studies programs represents a historical opportunity for the South to enter fully (not only in
literary ways) and on its own terms the twentieth century.
Further, there are specific elements of the southern experience as well as of this curricular process, that can provide
exemplars, both curricular and cultural for the rest of the
nation. These are suggested briefly by the following items:

1. As I envision these programs, they could provide
   an interesting study in confronting the American
   cultural dilemma specified by Christopher Lasch,
   namely, presentism, solipsism, political passivity,
   and ethical relativism. An interdisciplinary program
   in southern studies would be taught with the aim of
   reexperiencing denied elements of the past, which,
   when critically reintegrated, might help provide the
   psychology of social commitment, as well as remove
   "blocks" to the development of intelligence.

2. Given the Southern penchant for narrative and for
   place, political and cultural histories of the South
   can usefully and congruently be situated in life histories of individual students. The literature of autobiography provides an instructional method and
   agenda for this social psychoanalytic and educational process (Grumet 1988). Such pedogogical juxtaposition of the concrete and the abstract would
   provide a fascinating opportunity to study further
   the autobiographical experience of curriculum.

3. Individual autobiographical work needs to be com-
   plemented by group process. Groups led by specialists, and comprised by African-American and White
   men and women of varying class locations and sexual orientations would work to renegotiate in the interpersonal lived sphere, currently vertical and
   alienated, more horizontal and inclusive terms of social organization.

4. The relations among the past, the imagination, life
   history, collective experience, and the development
   of intelligence in its several modes can be specified
   and studied with select populations. Longitudinal

studies reminiscient of the Eight Year Study can provide important information regarding the extent to which these studies further, educationally and economically, those participating.

Southern Studies

Important aspects of this effort are already under way in higher education. These take the organizational forms of centers or institutes for southern studies. Among many northern scholars the concept of "southern studies" connotes a sentimentalization of the antebellum southern past. Programs so conceived would, of course, contribute to a continued repression of memory.

Fortunately, this "impression" is a stereotype. A review of program materials received from selected centers and institutes as well as visits to the two major educational units revealed a different reality. I found educational, research and service programs that express important elements of the curriculum theory as "place" described here. At both the Universities of Mississippi and South Carolina, for instance, I found collaboration with Afro-American and Women's Studies programs. Before describing the programs at these two institutions, permit me to review two more specialized centers.

The independent Institute for Southern Studies in Durham, North Carolina was founded in 1970 by veterans of the Civil Rights movement. It publishes the quarterly *Southern Exposure* and functions as a resource for community leaders, scholars, and others who work for social and economic change in the South. For instance, the Institute sponsored research and grassroots organizing activity that provoked regional struggles over utility rates, brown lung, capital punishment, toxic wastes, and workers' rights. These efforts resulted in citizen-based groups such as the Brown Lung Association, Southerners for Economic Justice, the Georgia Power Project, and the Gulf Coast Tenants Leadership Development Project. As well, the Institute has studied the South's contribution to American culture and social change, including gospel music, the blues, the Civil Rights movement and community organizing generally. The Institute offers no degrees. As of this writing (1989), Meredith Emmett is executive director; among those who sit on the Board of Directors is Julian Bond. Illustrative of Institute's interests include *Southern Exposure*'s recent reports on gay and lesbian life in the South and on relationships between the American South and South and Central America.

The Center for Southern History and Culture at the University of Alabama sponsors an Alabama state history magazine and journal called *"Heritage."* As of this writing, the Center offers no programs at the University nor does it support research fellows. Robert J. Norrell is director.

Two educational units—the Universities of South Carolin and Mississippi—offer academic programs and support a range of research and service programs. The programs of each expresses important curricular elements described earlier. (No endorsement of this essay by officials of either the Institute or the Center is implied, nor would I contend that my one-day visits to these campuses constitute an indepth curriculum evaluation).

The Institute for Southern Studies at the University of South Carolina existed in non-Institute form as early as the 1930s, although graduate programs waited until the 1980s. At the time southern studies was closely identified with the English department. An interdisciplinary Institute was founded in 1980. Professor of History Walter B. Edgar has served as director of the institute since its inception. Nancy Ashmore is assistant director.

Professor Edgar studied at Davidson College, coincidentally the same school where the Director of the other major southern studies unit—William Ferris of the University of Mississippi's Center for the Study of Southern Culture—also studied. Also coincidentally, both men adapted aspects of the interdisciplinary American and Afro-American studies programs at Yale in planning the Institute and Center, respectively.

An interdisciplinary major and minor are possible at South Carolina. Courses available to southern studies students include: Economic 329 (American Economic History), English 429A (Flannery O'Connor), History 631 (The Old South), History 649 (The Black Experience in the U.S. since 1865), Music 140 (Jazz and American Popular Music) as well as courses in Anthropology, Biology, Education, Geography, Geology, and Government. For a minor a student chooses eighteen (18) hours from among these offerings. For a major—a Bachelor of Arts in Interdisciplinary Studies—the student works with the curriculum coordinator of the Institute—Professor of Geography Charles Kovacik.

Graduate students in academic departments may be awarded assistantships by the Institute for Southern Studies to support related research. As well, research fellows from a variety of disciplines are supported. Publications and public events are also sponsored by the Institute.

The Institute collaborates with women's studies and with Afro-American studies in cosponsoring events. Courses in those areas are considered appropriate for southern studies majors and minors. There is no integrative seminar at the time of this writing, although Dr. Edgar was open to the idea when I posed the question during my April 1989 visit.

At that time I met with Di Anna Hyre, an undergraduate business major whose minor was southern studies. A bright and articulate student, Ms. Hyre undertook southern studies to support her business ambitions. She focused upon South Carolina history, particularly the influence of antebellum life upon contemporary life. As well, she had studied dialect differences among various groups of South Carolinians. Ms. Hyre was open as well to the integrative seminar idea; she supported my idea of extending southern studies at the university. Students from many disciplines enroll in southern studies courses. In this sense there is no "typical" student studying at the Institute.

I met as well with Professor Jack Ashley, a Flannery O'Connor scholar, with Professor Kovacik, a geographer and the institute's curriculum coordinator, and with Professor William H. Phillips, an economist whose course in American economic history provides opportunities to study southern economic history. The participating faculty are distinguished; the program is strong. Illustrative of the Institute's

interests include *South Carolina Women,* a slide presentation and guide prepared by Marcia G. Synnott.

In June 1989, I visited the Center for the Study of
Southern Culture at the University of Mississippi, directed
by William Ferris. After studying at Davidson College, Ferris took his M.A. in literature at Northwestern, followed by
a year at Trinity College Dublin, where he focussed upon the
work of James Joyce. After taking a Ph.D. in Folklore at the
University of Pennsylvania, Ferris taught two years at Jackson State—just after the 1970 killings—where he was close
to, among others, Alice Walker. Then Ferris went to Yale for
seven years, where he participated in the American and
Afro-American studies programs. He was selected to establish the Center for the Study of Southern Culture at the
University of Mississippi in 1977. Ferris is well-known as a
folklore scholar, filmmaker, and photographer. Author of
Blues from the Delta, coeditor of the *Encyclopedia of Southern Culture,* he is editor of *Folk Music and Modern Sound,
Afro-American Folk Art and Crafts* and *Local Color: Sense of
Place in Folk Art.* He served as Associate producer of *Mississippi Blues,* which was featured at the Cannes Film Festival.
As well, Dr. Ferris was a consultant to the *The Color Purple
and Crossroads.* His academic appointment at the University
is in the department of anthropology.

Both B.A. and M.A. programs in southern studies are
offered through the University of Mississippi Center for the
Study of Southern Culture. Team taught integrative semi-
nars open and close the undergradute and graduate course
of study. Among courses offered include nine courses in Afro-
American studies, anthropology, art history (two courses of
which are African and African-American focused), economics, English (two of the six offerings focus upon Black literature), music, political science, religion, sociology, theatre
arts, and a course on "Women in the South."

Among the research collections housed at the University
Library and used by scholars and students at the Center are
the Faulkner Collection, the world's largest blues archives,
B. B. King's record collection, and the Goldstein collection of
folklore. The *Encyclopedia of Southern Culture* is the first of

its kind. The Center publishes magazines on blues, gospel and country music as well as a newsletter, the combined readership of which numbers approximately 35,000. Each year the Center cosponsors a Faulkner conference (the 1989 theme was "Faulkner and Religion" and featured, among other speakers, Alfred Kazin and William Styron), and is at work establishing a video collection on the American South to be distributed by the Center.

One scholar affiliated with the Center is Robert Brinkmeyer, Jr., professor of literature and southern culture, who kindly met with me. Recently Brinkmeyer published a Bakhtinian study of the fiction of Flannery O'Connor. Entitled the *The Art and Vision of Flannery O'Connor* and published by the Louisiana State University Press, Brinkmeyer argues that O'Connor, as do dialogial writers, "open themselves up to their fiction." Bakhtin suggests that "one may enter into dialogue with the many voices of self. It's only by opening oneself up to dialogue that one may grow," suggests Professor Brinkmeyer. [Bakhtin's work has influenced curriculum theory (Whitson 1988); Brinkmeyer's use of it suggests a compatible curricular emphasis at Mississippi.] Brinkmeyer's future projects include a study of Katherine Porter and of southern writers'—especially Tate's and Ransom's—responses to the rise of world fascism in the 1930s.

The next decade, says Ferris, could be a time of extending southern studies to secondary schools. The Center has organized teacher institutes and published curricular materials, including: *Mississippi Writers: Reflections of Childhood and Youth, Volume I: Fiction, Volume II: Non-Fiction,* and *Volume III: Poetry,* all edited by Dorothy Abbott. Regionally thematized projects are possible.

In my view, the Institute for Southern Studies at the University of South Carolina and the more ambitious University of Mississippi Center for the Study of Southern Culture constitute major expressions of the educational and cultural effort I envision. They might well serve as models for similar centers at each of the major research universities of the South. As well, the development of curricular materials and the education of teachers ought to be undertaken, as the educational significance of southern studies makes them appropriate study in elementary and secondary schools. The rate of educational failure in the South speaks of a psychosocial and cultural estrangement which southern studies programs like those of the Universities of Mississippi and South Carolina can undertake to articulate, understand, and perhaps heal.

Postscript

Students of curriculum theory will recognize here employment of several strands of contemporary curriculum research: the political, the autobiographical, the phenomenological and the gender-focused. Interdisciplinary courses that draw upon students' prior knowledge as well as referring to new knowledge in various disciplines represent sound practice of curriculum theory, particularly when these abstract traditions are then situated in the concrete lives of individuals and groups. Curriculum in this sense becomes a place of origin as well as destination, a ground from which intelligence can develop, and a figure for presenting new perceptions and reviewing old ones. Curriculum as a southern place is also the study of absence, the admission of denial, the integration of the culturally excluded (race), the denied (class) and bifurcated (gender). Obviously the obstacles are many and jagged; only an institutional effort generously supported could proceed with even modest expectations of success. Such an effort will be worth the investment, I would suggest. The effort, writ large, represents the conscious cultivation of a truly New South.

Appendix: Regional Studies Centers*

Alabama

Center for Southern History and
    Southern Culture   205–348–7467
University of Alabama
Box CS, 2400 Brycelawn
Tuscaloosa, AL 34587

Alaska

[Studies of Special Interest Groups
    and Sectionalism]   907–789–4404
Department of Political Science
University of Alaska at Juneau
Juneau, AK 99801

Arizona

Mexican American Studies &
    Research Center   Est. 1981
204 Modern Languages Building   606–621–5121
University of Arizona
Tucson, AZ 85721

The Southwest Center   Est. 1986
Library C327   602–621–2484
University of Arizona
Tucson, AZ 85721

---

*   Courtesy of Dr. Glen Lich, Director Center for Regional Studies, Baylor
University, Waco, Texas.

Arkansas

Center for Arkansas and Regional Studies   Est. 1981
Suite 12 Oak Hall   501–575–3001
University of Arkansas
Fayetteville, AR

Center for Arkansas Studies
University of Arkansas, Little Rock   501–569–8782
College of Liberal Arts
33rd & University
Little Rock, AR

California

Sacramento Valley Study   Est. 1977
University of California, Davis
Davis, CA 95616

El Colegio de la Frontera Norte
P.O. Box L
Chula Vista, CA 92010

Center for U.S.-Mexican Studies   Est. 1980
University of California, San Diego   619–534–4503
D–010, La Jolla, CA 92093

Center for Pacific Rim Studies
2130 Fulton Street
San Francisco, CA 94117–1080

Conference on Interdisciplinary Education
Department of History   619–265–5262
College of Arts and Letters
San Diego State University
San Diego, CA 92182

Institute for Regional Studies   Est. 1983
   of the Californias   619–265–5423
San Diego State University
San Diego, CA 92182

Florida

Hemispheric Policy Studies Center
300 N.E. 2nd Avenue
Miami, FL 33132

Hawaii

School of Hawaiian, Asian   Est. 1931
  and Pacific Studies   808–948–8324
1890 East–West Road
Moore Hall 315
University of Hawaii at Manoa
Honolulu, HI 96822

Idaho

The Snake River Regional Studies Center   Est. 1975
The College of Idaho   208–459–5214
2112 Cleveland Blvd.
Caldwell, ID 83605–9990

Illinois

Committee on Geographical Studies   312–702–8308
University of Chicago
Chicago, IL 60637

Kansas

Center for Great Plains Studies   Est. 1978
Emporia State University   316–343–1200
Emporia, KS 66801

Kentucky

Center for Intercultural and Folk Studies
Western Kentucky University   502–745–4295
Bowling Green, KY 42101

The Appalachian Center   Est. 1977
University of Kentucky   606–257–4852
641 South Limestone
Lexington, KY 40506

Louisiana

Center for Louisiana Studies   Est. 1973
The University of Southwest Louisiana   318–231–6029
Lafayette, LA 70504

Louisiana Folklife Center   Est. 1976
Northwest State University of LA   318–357–4332
Natchitoches, LA 71497

Red River Regional Studies Center
Louisiana State University
  in Shreveport   318–797–5332
One University Place
Shreveport, LA 71115

Massachusetts

Centers for New England Culture
University of Massachusettes, Amherst   413–545–2158
Amherst, MA 01003

Maine

Center for New England Studies   Est. 1987
University of Southern Maine   207–780–4920
Gorham, ME 04038

Canadian-American Center   Est. 1987
Canada House, 154 College Aven   207–581–1506
University of Maine
Orono, ME 04469

Minnesota

[American Studies: Regional Studies
  Concentration]   612–624–1658
14 Scott Hall
72 Pleasant Street, SE
University of Minnesota
Minneapolis, MN 55455–0225

Mississippi

Center for the Study of the Southern Culture
The University of Mississippi   601–232–5993
University, MS 38677

The School of Architecture
The Center for Small Town Research and Design
Mississippi State University
School of Art
Mississippi State, MS 39762

Missouri

Missouri Cultural Heritage Center
University of Missouri—Columbia   314–882–6296
Graduate School and Office of Research
Columbia, MO 65211

Center for the Ozarks
Southwest Missouri State University   417–836–5000
901 South National
Springfield, MO 65804

Nebraska

Center for Great Plains Studies
University of Nebraska, Lincoln   402–472–6058
Lincoln, NE 68588–0314

North American Prairie Project
University of Nebraska, Omaha   402–554–2641
Omaha, NE 68182–0040

New Jersey

Center for the American Woman
  and Politics   Est. 1971
Eagleton Institute of Politics   201–828–2210
Rutgers, The State University
  of New Jersey
New Brunswick, NJ 08901

School of Urban and Regional Policy
Urban Studies Department   201–932–4101
Rutgers University
New Brunswick, NJ 08903

Council on Regional Studies   Est. 1961
Princeton University
Princeton, NJ 08544

Department of History   201–932–8993
Rutgers University
New Brunswick, NJ 08903

New Mexico

The Institute of the North American West
University of New Mexico
Albuquerque, NM 87106

The New Mexico Heritage Center
Department of English/Box 3E
New Mexico State University
Las Cruces, NM 88003

Center for Latin American Studies   Est. 1979
New Mexico State University   505–646–3524
Nason House
1200 University Avenue
Campus Box 3JBR
Las Cruces, NM 88003

North Carolina

Center for the Improvement of Mountain Living
Western Carolina University
Bird Building
Cullowhee, NC 28723

Center for Urban and Regional Studies
Campus Box 3410, Hickerson House   919–962–3074
University of North Carolina at Chapel Hill
Chapel Hill, NC 27599

Department of City and Regional Planning   Est. 1946
New East 033A   919–962–5204
University of North Carolina at Chapel Hill
Chapel Hill, NC 27514

Center for Appalachian Studies   Est. 1978
Appalachian State University   704–262–4089
Boone, NC 28608

Institute for Southern Studies   Est. 1978
P.O. Box 531   919–688–8167
Durham, NC 27702

Ohio

Center for Neighborhood and Community Studies
University of Cincinnati
Cincinnati, OH 45221

Institute for Great Lakes Research
Bowling Green State University
Bowling Green, OH 43403

Byrd Polar Research Center
The Ohio State University
Columbus, OH 43210

Program for Regional and Comparative History
Case Western Reserve University   216–368–2381
Cleveland, OH 44106

Pennsylvania

Center for Pennsylvania German Studies   Est. 1986
Byerly Hall   717–872–3539
Millersville University
Millersville, PA 17551

Regional American Studies Center   Est. 1988
Pennsylvania State University   717–948–6039
U.S. Route 230
Middletown, PA 17057

Center for Philadelphia Studies
University of Pennsylvania
Philadelphia, PA 19104–8387

South Carolina

Southern Regional Science Association
225 Barre Hall   803–656–5761
Clemson University
Clemson, SC 29632

Institute for Southern Studies   Est. 1980
University of South Carolina   803–777–2340
Columbia, SC 29208

South Dakota

Center for Western Studies   Est. ca. 1965
Augustana College   605–336–4007
Box 727
Sioux Falls, SD 57197

Texas

Baylor University   Est. 1985
Center for Regional Studies   817–755–2190

CSB Box 696
Waco, TX 76798

University of Texas
Institute of Texan Cultures at San Antonio
P.O. Box 1226
San Antonio, TX 78294

The Great Plains Institute
West Texas State University   806–656–0111
Canyon, TX 79016

Center for Big Bend Studies
Box C –71   915–837–8149
Sul Ross State University
Alpine, TX 79832

Chihuahuan Desert Symposium
P.O. Box 1334   915–837–8370
Alpine, TX 79832

Center for Texas Studies
North Texas State University   817–565–2000
Denton, TX 76203

Center for Inter-American and Border Studies
University of Texas at El Paso   915–747–5196
El Pasco, TX 79968

Institute for German-Texan Studies
Center for German Area Studies   713–749–2159
University of Houston
Houston, TX

Southwest Borderlands Center
Association of Borderland Studies   512–595–3503
Kingsville, TX 78363

Center for Multicultural and Gender Studies
Southwest Texas State University   512–245–3630
San Marcos, TX 78666

Utah

Mountain West Center for Regional Studies   Est. 1986
Utah State University   801–750–3630
Logan, UT 84322–0735

Charles Redd Center for Western Studies   Est. 1978
Brigham Young University   801-378-4048
4069 Harold B. Lee Library
Provo, UT 84602

Vermont

Center for Research in Vermont
Lake Champlain Research Study   802-656-3180
Winooki,VT 05404

The Center for Northern Studies
Wolcott, VT 05680   802-888-4331

Washington, D.C.

Center for Washington Area Study   Est. 1980
George Washington University
Washington, D.C. 20052

Wisconsin

Max Kade Institute for German-American Studies
University of Wisconsin   608-262-7546
Madison, WI 53705

Wyoming

Center for Rocky Mountain Culture Studies
American Studies Program
301 Hoyt Hall
University of Wyoming
Laramie, WY 82071

Buffalo Bill Historical Center
P.O. Box 1000   307-587-4771
Cody, WY 82414

Austria

Institute for English and American Studies
University of Vienna
Lammgasse 8
1-1080 Vienna, Austria

Canada

School of Community and Regional Planning
University of British Columbia
6333 Memorial Road   604–228–3276
Vancouver, British Columbia V6T 1W5

Canadian Plains Research Center
University of Regina   306–585–4758

Gorsebrook Research Institute for Atlantic
Canada Studies   902–429–9780

Saint Mary's University
Halifax, Nova Scotia B3H 3C3

Institute for Northern Ontario
Research and Development   706–675–1151

Laurentian University
Ramsey Lake Road
Sudbury, Ontario P3E 2G8

Center for Urban and Community Studies
University of Toronto   416–978–2072
455 Spadina Avenue
Toronto, Ontario M5S 2G8

Canadian Institute for Research
  on Regional Development
University of Moncton
Local 292
Edifice Taillon
Moncton, New Brunswick E1A 3E9

Institut National de la Recherche
Scientifique-Urbanisation   514–842–4191
University of Quebec
3465 Durocher
Montreal, PQ H2X 2C6

Institute for Canadian-American Studies
University of Windsor   519–253–4232
Windsor, Ontario N9B 3P4

North American Studies Program
McGill University   514–398–4455

845 Sherbrooke Street
Montreal, Quebec H3A 2T5

Center for American Studies
University of Western Ontario   519–679–2111
London, Ontario NGA 3K7
Regional and Urban Studies Centre
Halifax, NS, Canada

Center for Northern Studies and Research
McGill University   514–398–4961
Montreal, PQ, Canada H3A 1BG

Northern and Native Studies
Institute of Canadian Studies   613–564–2873
Ottawa, ON, Canada

United Kingdom

School of Scottish Studies
University of Edinburgh
27 George Square
Edinburgh EH8 9LD
Scotland
United Kingdom

West Germany

West Germany
   Historishes Seminar

West Germany
Landesinstitut Schleswig Holstein
Ferdinana-Sauerbruch-Strasse 2   048–217–8240
D–2210 Itzehoe
West Germany

Heimatselle Pfalz
Benzinoring 6   0631–93362
D–6750 Kaiserslautern
West Germany

Tuebinger Institut fuer empirische
Soziologie und Heimatkunde

Universitaet Tuebingen
West Germany

Center for North American
Studies and Research
Guender 11
Frankfort University
Federal Republic of Germany

Notes

Introduction

1. George Garrett, "Southern Literature Here and Now." In Fifteen Southerners, *Why The South Will Survive* (Athens, Georgia: University of Georgia Press, 1981).

Chapter 1.

All letters and other primary sources used in these references may be found in Special Collections, Hoskins Library, and The University of Tenneessee, Knoxville.

1. Margaret Anderson, *The Children of the South,* (New York: 1958).

2. Edwin A. Alderman, "The Child and the State," *Proceedings of the Fifth Conference for Education in the South* (1902): 75.

3. *Proceedings of the Seventh Conference for Education in the South* (1904): 173.

4. Clinton B. Allison, "Training Dixie's Teachers: The University of Tennessee," *Three School of Education: Approaches to Institutional History,* Ayres Bagley, ed., Society of Professors of Education Monograph Series, 1984.

5. Clinton B. Allison, "Early Professors of Education: Three Case Studies," *The Professors of Teaching: An Inquiry,* Richard Wisniewski and Edward R. Ducharme, eds., (New York: 1989).

6. Hoke Smith, "Popular Education as the Primary Policy of the South," *Proceedings of the Fifth Conference for Education in the South* (1902): 43.

7. T. G. Bush, *Proceedings of the Seventh Conference for Education in the South* (1904): 10.

8. Charles William Dabney, *Universal Education in the South*, (Chapel Hill, North Carolina: 1936).

9. Clarence Karier, "American Educational History: A Perspective." Paper presented at the annual meeting of the Southern History of Education Society, Atlanta, November 1971; James D. Anderson, *The Education of Blacks in the South*, 1860–1945, (Chapel Hill, North Carolina: 1988); Clinton B. Allison, "The Conference of Education in the South: An Exercise in Noblesse Oblige," *Journal of Thought* (Summer 1981).

10. Robert S. Cotterill, "The Old South and the New," *The Pursuit of Southern History: Presidential Addresses of the Southern Historical Association, 1935–1936* (Baton Rouge, Louisiana: 1936), P. 238.

11. Kathleen P. Bennett, "MacArthur High School Today: The Construction of Class." Paper presented to the Southwest Philosophy of Education Society, (November 1988), 6. Much of the education on Farragut School today is from an ethnographic study being conducted by Bennett.

12. Ibid., 13.

13. Ibid., 1.

14. My understanding of the country life movement came primarily from William L. Bowers, *The Country Life Movement In America, 1900–1920* (Port Washington, N.Y.: 1975); and James H. Madison, "John D. Rockefeller's General Education Board and the Rural School Problem in the Midwest, 1900–1930," *History of Education Quarterly* 24 (Summer 1984).

15. Knoxville Sentinel, 28 June 1936.

16. Knoxville Journal and Tribune, 16 September 1902.

17. Washington, D.C.: U.S. Bureau of Education Bulletin No. 49, 1913.

18. Charles Dabney to S. L. Chesnutt, Jr., (21 February 1903).

19. Knoxville Journal and Tribune, 3 May 1902.

20. Knoxville Journal and Tribune, 24 July 1903.

21. Dabney to S. L. Chesnutt, Jr., (21 February 1903) and Dabney, "letter of support," (9 October 1905).

22. Philander P. Claxton to Mari Hofer, (21 April 1905).

23. Amanda Stoltzfus to Dabney, (2 February 1903).

24. Dabney to Stoltzfus, (30 March 1906).

25. Stoltzfus to Miss Fain, (16 June 1906).

26. Farragut *Announcement*, (1911–12): 48.

27. Elbert Hubbard, "A 'Modified Montessori,' " (3 April 1914) Knoxville Sentinel.

28. Ibid.

29. Ibid.

30. Farragut *Announcement*, (1911–12): 19.

31. Hubbard, "A 'Modified Montessori.' "

32. Dabney to Samuel L. Chesnutt, Jr., (14 October 1905).

33. Chesnutt to Dabney, (17 October 1905).

34. Stoltzfus to Fain, (16 June 1906).

35. Farragut *Announcement*, (1911–12): 46.

36. Hubbard.

37. Farragut *Announcement*, (1906–07).

38. Hubbard.

39. Farragut *Announcement*, (1906–07).

40. Hubbard.

41. Stoltzfus to Dabney, (18 January 1906).

42. Washington, D.C.: U.S. Bureau of Education Bulletin, 8.

43. Farragut *Announcement*, (1911–12): 46.

44. Ibid., 16–17.

45. Knoxville Sentinel, 24 July, 1903.

46. Washington, D.C.: U.S. Bureau of Education Bulletin, 14 and 15.

47. Farragut *Announcement,* (1911–12).

48. Chesnutt to Dabney, (17 October 1905).

49. Farragut *Announcement,* (1911–12): 46.

50. Farragut *Announcement,* (1906–07).

51. Ibid.

52. Roy Earl Graham, "Vocational, Educational, and Social Status of Graduates and Non-Graduates of Farragut High School," Master of Science thesis, The University of Tennessee, 1933.

Chapter 2.

1. *Mobile v. Bolden,* 446 U.S. 55 (1980); *Wallace V. Jaffree,* 472 U.S. 38 (1985); *Smith v. Board of School Comm'rs,* 827 F.2d 684 (11th Cir. 1987).

2. For the early history of Mobile, see Harriet E. Amos, *Cotton City: Urban Development in Antebellum Mobile* (Tuscaloosa: University of Alabama Press, 1985); and Michael Thomason and Melton McLaurin, *Mobile: American River City* (Mobile: Easter Publishing, 1975).

3. *Engel V. Vitale,* 370 U.S. 421(1962); *School Dist. of Abington Township v. Schempp,* 374 U.S. 203 (1963). In 1987, 68 percent of Americans favored "an amendment to the U.S. Constitution that would allow prayer in the public schools" according to Alec M. Gallup and David L. Clark, "The 19th Annual Gallup Poll of the Public's Attitudes toward the Schools," *Phi Delta Kappan* 69 (September 1987): 24–25.

4. *Jaffree v. Board of School Comm'rs,* 554 F.Supp. 1104, 1107 (S.D. Ala. 1983).

5. Ibid.

6. Id. at 1107–08.

7. ALA. CODE sec. 16–1–20.2 (Supp. 1984). Emphasis in the original.

8. *Mobile Register,* July 1, July 13, 1982. The *Mobile Register* will hereafter be cited as *Register.*

9. Interview with Ishmael Jaffree, Mobile, April 20, 1985. Unless otherwise cited, all quotations from Jaffree are from the interview.

10. *Register,* August 3, 1982.

11. ALA. CODE sec. 16–1–20.1 (Supp. 1984).

12. *Jaffree v. James,* 554 F. Supp. 727, 729 (S.D Ala. 1982).

13. *Register,* August 3, 1982.

14. Ibid.

15. *Jaffree v. James,* 554 F. Supp. at 727–28.

16. Brief for ACLU, *amicus curiae,* at 8, *Jaffree v. Wallace,* 705 F. 2d 1526 (11th Cir. 1983).

17. *Mobile Press-Register,* September 19, 1982. The *Mobile Press-Register* will hereafter be cited as *Press-Register.*

18. *Jaffree v. James,* 554 F. Supp. at 732 n.2.

19. Id. at 732.

20. Id. at 733.

21. Ibid. Judge Hand divided Jaffree's complaint into two cases, one relating to the state laws and the other relating to the teachers' activities.

22. *School Law News,* September 24, 1982.

23. Ibid.

24. *Register,* September 24, 1982.

25. *Register,* November 16, 1982.

26. *Register,* November 18, 1982.

27. *Everson v. Board of Educ.,* 330 U.S. 1 (1947).

28. *Register,* November 18, 1982.

29. *Register,* November 17, November 19, 1982.

30. *Register,* November 17, 1982.

31. *Register,* November 17–19, 1982.

32. *Register,* November 21, 1982.

33. *Register,* November 18, 1982.

34. *Register,* November 19, 1982.

35. *Torcaso v. Watkins,* 367 U.S. 488, 495 n.11 (1961).

36. *Register,* November 19, 1982.

37. *Jafreee v. Board of School Comm'rs,* 554 F. Supp. at 1128.

38. Id. at 1129 n.41.

39. Id. at 1130 n.41.

40. Id. at 1129 n.41.

41. Id. at 1118 n.24.

42. Since Judge Hand found no violation of the U.S. Constitution in *Jaffree v. Board of School Comm'rs,* the case involving teacher-initiated prayer, he also dismissed *Jaffree v. James,* 554 F. Supp. 1130 (S.D. Ala. 1983), the case involving state prayer laws.

43. *Register,* February 17, 1983.

44. *Press-Register,* January 15, 1983.

45. *Press-Register,* January 16, 1983.

46. *Press-Register,* January 15, 1983.

47. *Register,* August 19, 1983.

48. *Education USA,* February 21, 1983.

49. *Jaffree v. Board of School Comm'rs,* 103 S. Ct. 842 (1983) (Powell, Cir. J.).

50. *Register,* February 18, May 3, 1983.

51. *Jaffree v. Wallace,* 705 f.2d 1526 (11th Cir. 1983).

52. *Jaffree v. Wallace,* 713 F.2d 614 (11th Cir. 1983).

53. See summaries, 52, U.S.L.W. 3557, 3557–58 (U.S. Jan. 24, 1984) (Nos. 83–804, 83–812, 83–929).

54. *Wallace v. Jaffree,* 52 U.S.L.W. 3719 (U.S. Apr. 2, 1984).

55. *Register,* June 5, 1985.

56. *Wallace v. Jaffree,* 472 U.S. 38, 59 (1985).

57. Id. at 38–39.

58. Id. at 73–74.

59. Id. at 55, quoting *Board of Educ. v. Barnette,* 319 U.S. 624, 642 (1943).

60. *Wallace v. Jaffree,* 472 U.S. at 55.

61. Id. at 90.

62. Id. at 113.

63. *Register,* June 5, 1985.

64. *Register,* June 11, 1985.

65. *Register,* June 7, 1985.

66. *Register,* June 5, 1985.

67. *Smith v. Board of School Comm'rs,* 655 F. Supp. 939, 943–44 (S.D. Ala. 1987).

68. *Mobile Press,* October 6, 1986. The *Mobile Press* will hereafter be cited as *Press.*

69. See stories in the *Press, Register,* and *Press-Register,* October 6–22, 1986.

70. *Press-Register,* October 19, 1986.

71. *Smith v. Board of School Comm'rs,* 655 F. Supp. at 988.

72. *Smith v. Board of School Comm'rs,* 827 F.2d 684, 692 (11th Cir. 1987).

73. Id. at 689.

74. *Register,* June 1, 1989.

75. *Register,* August 27, 1987.

76. *Press-Register,* October 25, 1986.

77. Ibid.

78. Kirsten Goldberg, "Alabama Group Closes Its 'Secular Humanism' Suit," *Education Week,* December 9, 1987.

79. All quotations are from the PBS series "We the People" (1987), Episode One: "Free To Believe."

Chapter 3.

1. Martin, Biddy, and Mohanty, Chandra T. (1986). "Feminist Politics: What's Home Got to Do with It?" In T. deLauretis, ed. *Feminist Studies Critical Studies*, 191–212. Bloomington, IN: Indiana University Press.

2. Robert Hodge and Gunther Kress, *Social Semiotics* Ithaca: Cornell University Press, 1988, p. 86. Stereotyping has been classed an "accent of an accent" by Hodge and Kress. The discussion is repeated here.

> They [stereotypes] are the selection, inflection and reading of a whole system of accents by a hostile community, a recuperation of the deviancy of the accent by reducing it to something simple, manageable and under the control of people outside the accent-community. So English speakers fancy their "Irish" accent, American do their "Negro" take-off, and Australians are delighted with their Aboriginal imitations. In each case, the real accent expresses the identity of the community, and excludes all other speakers. The stereotype constitutes the counter-claim that membership of that speech community is easy but worthless.

3. Friere, Paulo. 1970. Pedagogy for the Oppressed. New York: Seabury Press; and Giroux, Henry A. 1988. *Schooling and the Struggle for Public Life: Critical Pedagogy in the Modern Age*, 147–72, Minneapolis: The University of Minnesota Press.

4. Ibid., p. 152.

5. Ibid., p. 155.

6. Ibid., p. 160–1.

7. James Baldwin, *No Name In the Streets:* 1972, p. 66.

8. Maya Angelou, *I Know Why The Caged Bird Sings* (New York: Random House, 1969), p. 231.

9. Ibid., p. 7.

10. Ibid., p. 128.

11. Maya Angelou, *Singin' and Swingin' and Gettin' Merry Like Christmas* (New York: Bantam Books, 1976), p. 26.

12. Tracy Chapman: 1986. "Fast Car," from her album *Tracy Chapman*. New York: Elektra/Asylum Records.

13. Sondra O'Neale, "Reconstruction of the Composit Self: New Images of Black Women in Maya Angelou's Continuing Autobiography." In M. Evans, ed., *Black Women Writers (1950–1980): A Critical Evaluation* (Garden City New York: Anchor Press/Doubleday, 1984) p.26.

14. Maya Angelou, *I Know Why the Caged Bird Sings*, p.2.

15. Maya Angelou, pp. 100–101.

16. Minnie Bruce Pratt, "Identity: Skin Blood Heart." 1984. In E. Bulkin, M. B. Pratt, and B. Smith, *Yours in Struggle: Three Feminist Perspectives on Anti-Semitism and Racism*, 11–63. Brooklyn: Long Haul Press.

17. Maya Angelou, 1974, p. 62.

18. Gary P. Nunn, "The London Homesick Blues." From the Lost Gonzo Band album, *Signs of Life*. 1978. Capitol EMI, first published by Nunn Publishing, BMI, 1973.

19. Pratt, p. 41.

20. William Pinar, 1988. " 'Whole, Bright, Deep With Understanding': Issues in Qualitative Research and Autobiographical Method." In his *Contemporary Curriculum Discourses*, 134–153. Scottsdale, AZ: Gorsuch Scarisbrick.

Chapter 4.

1. "The New Appalachian Subregions and Their Development Strategies," *Appalachia*, Vol. 8, no. 1 (August-September 1974), pp. 10–27.

2. Loyal Jones, (1975), pp. 509–510.

3. Denise Giardina, *Storming Heaven* (New York: Ivey Books, 1987), p. 291.

4. Ibid., p. 89, 121.

5. Wilma Dykeman, *Tall Woman* (New York: Holt, Rinehart, 1962), p. 207, 278.

6. Giardina, *Storming Heaven*, p. 48.

7. Ibid., p. 129.

8. James Still, *River of Earth* (1940; reprint, Lexington, KY: University of Kentucky Press, 1978), pp. 51–52.

9. Giardina, *Storming Heaven,* p. 227.

10. Wendall Berry, *The Memory of Old Jack* (New York: Harcourt Brace Joanovich, 1974), p. 13.

11. Wendall Berry, *I Am One of You Forever:* (1974) p. 169.

12. Giardino, *Storming Heaven,* pp. 18, 20.

13. Ibid., p. 24.

14. Ibid., p. 77.

15. Harriette Cunou, *The Dollmaker* (New York: Macmillan Company, 1954), pp. 24–25. In this example, Gertie was on her way to the town's doctor with her seriously ill baby. She had cut his neck in order to clear an obstruction in his windpipe, allowing him to breathe.

16. Lee Smith, *Black Mountain Breakdown* (New York: Ballantine Books, 1980), p. 25.

17. Berry, *I Am One of You . . . ,* p. 144, 143.

18. Student paper, "Schooling in Appalachia" class, University of Tennessee.

19. Student paper, "Schooling in Appalachia" class, University of Tennessee.

Chapter 5.

1. Roland Barthes, *Mythologies* (New York: Hill and Wang, 1972), pp. 142–43.

2. Eric Fromm, *The Heart of Man* (New York: Harper and Row, 1980), p. 79.

3. Willie Morris, *Terrains of the Heart* (Oxford Miss: Yoknapatawpha Press, 1981), pp. 30–31.

4. Willie Morris, *North Toward Home* (Oxford, Miss: Yoknapatawpha Press, 1967), p. 77.

5. Ibid., p. 77–78.

6. Ibid., p. 40–43, 52–54.

7. Ibid., p. 135, 140–41.

8. Ibid., p. 141–42.

9. Ibid., p. 153.

10. Ibid., p. 139–140.

11. Ibid., p. 123.

12. Ibid., 179–80.

13. Ibid., 121.

14. Morris, *Terrains of the Heart,* p. 230.

15. Richard Gray, *Writing the South* (New York: Cambridge University Press, 1986).

16. Morris, *Terrains of the Heart,* p. 242.

Chapter 6.

1. C. G. Sellers, *The Southerner as American* (Chapel Hill: Univesity of North Carolina Press, 1960), p. vi.

2. Thomas Dixon, *The Leopard's Spots: A Romance of the White Man's Burden* (New York: 1902), pp. 5, 33.

3. K. Fishburn, *Women in Popular Culture: A Reference Guide* (Conn: Greenwood Press, 1982), pp. 10–11.

4. W. King, "South Leads the Country in School Desegregation," *The New York Times,* p. A16.

5. A. M. Garibaldi, *The Decline of Teacher Production in Louisiana* (Louisiana: Southern Education Foundation, 1986), p. 10.

6. Scott Jasckik, "Case Charging Mississippi Had a Segregated System of Higher Education is Dismissed by a Federal Judge." *Chronicle of Higher Education,* January 6, 1988, p. A22.

7. A. Karnig and P. McClain, "The New South and Black Economic and Political Development: Changes from 1970 to 1980." *The Western Political Quarterly,* 38, p. 540.

8. Ibid., p. 544–545.

9. M. W. Apple, "The Culture and Commerce of the Textbook." In William Pinar, ed., *Contemporary Curriculum Discourses* (Scottsdale, AZ: Gorsuch Scarisbrick, 1988), p. 225.

10. D. B. Fleming, "A Review of Slave Life in Fourteen United States History Textbooks." *Journal of Negro Education,* 56, No. 4, p. 556.

11. Sue Eaken and M. Culbertson, *Louisiana: The Land and Its People,* p. 272.

12. Ibid., p. 275.

13. H. Dethloff, and A. Bognaud, *Our Louisiana Legacy* (LA: Steck Vaughn Co., 1980), p. 205.

14. K. J. Winkler, "Scholars Extend Definition of Southern Culture by Including History of Blacks, Ethnic Groups," *The Chronicle of Higher Education,* January 27, 1988, p. A9.

15. W. F. Pinar, *Contemporary Curriculum Discourses,* (Scottsdale, AZ: Gorsuch Scarisbrick, 1988), p. 273.

Chapter 7.

1. David Potter, *The South and the Sectional Conflict* (Baton Rouge: Louisiana State University Press, 1968).

2. William Faulkner, *Intruder in the Dust* (New York: Random House, 1948).

Bibliography

Angelou, Maya. 1969. *I Know Why the Caged Bird Sings.* New York: Random House.

———. 1974. *Gather Together in My Name.* New York: Random House.

———. 1976. *Singin' and Swingin' and Gettin' Merry Like Christmas.* New York: Bantam Books.

———. 1981. *The Heart of a Woman.* New York: Bantam Books.

Anon. "The New Appalachian Subregions and Their Development Strategies," *Appalachia,* Vol. 8, No. 1 (August-September, 1974), pp. 10–27.

Apple, M. W. (1988). "The Culture and Commerce of the Textbook." In William Pinar, ed., *Contemporary Curriculum Discourses.*

Arnow, Harriette. 1954. *The Dollmaker.* New York: The Macmillan Company.

Baldwin, James. 1972. *No Name in the Streets* as quoted in Benjamin Demott, "James Baldwin on the Sixties: Acts and Revelations." *Saturday Review,* 55 (May 27):66.

Barthes, Roland. 1972. *Mythologies.* New York: Hill and Wang.

Berghe, van den P. 1967. *Race and Racism.* New York: John Wiley & Sons.

Berry, Wendell. 1974. *The Memory of Old Jack.* New York: Harcourt Brace Jovanovich.

Bettersworth, J. K. 1974. *Your Mississippi.*

Billings, Dwight. 1989. "Appalachians." In *Encyclopedia of Southern Culture.* Charles R. Wilson and William Ferris, eds. Chapel Hill, NC: University of North Carolina Press.

Brown, Rita Mae. 1987. "Surrender to Life." *Free Inquiry* 7 (Summer):38–40.

Bullock, Henry A. 1967. *A History of Negro Education in the South: From 1619 to the Present.* Cambridge, MA: Harvard University Press.

Carter, D. T. 1981. From the Old South to the New. In Walter Fraser & Winfred Moore, eds., *From the Old South to the New: Essays on the Transitional South* Connecticut: Greenwood Press.

Cash, W. J. 1941. *The Mind of the South.* New York: Alfred Knopf.

Chapell, Fred. 1985. *I am One of You Forever.* Baton Rouge, LA: Louisiana State University Press.

Cleaver, Eldridge. 1968. *Soul on Ice.* New York: MacGraw Hill.

Clement, Richard. 1983. *Northernizing The South.* Athens, GA: University of Georgia Press.

Cohen, S. 1988. Mississippi Town Symbolized Black Political Progress. *The Times Picayune,* March 27, p.A–5.

Collingwood, R. G. 1962. *The Idea of History.* New York: Oxford University Press.

Cooper, William J. Jr. 1978. *The South and the Politics Of Slavery 1826–1956.* Baton Rouge, LA: Louisiana State University Press.

Dabbs, James McBride. 1964. *Who Speaks For The South?* New York: Funk & Wagnalls Company, Inc.

Davenport, F. Garvin. 1967. *The Myth of Southern History.* Nashville, TN: Vanderbilt University Press.

Dethloff, H. & Begnaud, A. 1980. *Our Louisiana Legacy.* LA: Steck Vaughn Co.

Dixon, T. 1902. *The Leopard's Spots: A Romance of the White Man's Burden.* New York: Press.

Donald, D. H. 1981. A Generation of Defeat. In Walter Fraser & Winfred Moore, eds., *From the Old South to the New: Essays on the Transitional South. CT. Greenwood Press*

Dugas, Lynda S. and Cheryl J. Edwards. 1988. "Preparing Riders for the 'Second Wave': Or Learning How to 'Hang Ten' in

Elementary Methods." Paper presented at the tenth conference on curriculum theory and classroom practice, Dayton, Ohio.

Dykeman, Wilma. 1973. *Tall Woman*. 1962 Reprint. New York: Holt, Rinehart.

Eakin, S. & Culbertson, M. 1986. *Louisiana: The Land and Its People*. LA: Pelican Publisher.

Eisner, E. W. 1979. *The Educational Imagination: On the Design and Evaluation of School Programs*. New York: MacMillan.

Elkins, Stanley. 1968. *Slavery: A Problem in American Institutional and Intellectual Life*. Chicago IL: University of Chicago Press.

Evans, Mari, ed. 1984. *Black Women Writers (1950–1980): A Critical Evaluation*. Garden City, New York: Anchor Press/Doubleday.

Faulkner, William. 1946. *The Sound and the Fury*. New York: Vintage Books.

———. 1948. *Intruder in the Dust*. New York: Random House.

———. 1960. *Go Down Moses*. London: Random House.

Fishburn, K. 1982. *Women in Popular Culture: A Reference Guide*. CT: Greenwood Press.

Fleming, D. B. 1987. A Review of Slave Life in Fourteen United States History Textbooks. *Journal of Negro Education 56*, no. 4, 550–556.

Fox-Genovese, E. 1988. *Within the Plantation Household: Black and White Women of the Old South*. Chapel Hill, NC: University of North Carolina Press.

Franklin, J. H. 1960. As For Our History. In Charles Sellers, ed., *The Southerner as American*. Chapel Hill, NC: The University of North Carolina Press.

Fredrickson, G. M. 1971. *The Black Image in the White Mind*. New York: Harper and Row.

Freyre, Gilberto. 1963. *New World in the Tropics*. New York: Vintage Books.

Freire, Paulo. 1970. *Pedagogy for the Oppressed*. New York: Seabury Press.

————. *The Politics of Education*. South Hadley, MA: Bergin and Garvey Publishers

Freire, Paulo and Donaldo Macedo. 1987. *Literacy: Reading the Word and the World*. South Hadley, MA: Bergin and Garvey Publishers.

Fromm, Eric. 1980. *The Heart of Man*. New York: Harper and Row.

Gardner, Howard. 1983. *Frames of Mind: The Theory of Multiple Intelligences*. New York: Basic Books.

Garibaldi, A. M. 1986. *The Decline of Teacher Production in Louisiana* (1976–83). Southern Education Foundation.

Garrett, George. 1981. "Southern Literature Here and Now." In Fifteen Southerners, *Why the South Will Survive*. Athens, GA: University of Georgia Press.

Genovese, Eugene D. 1964. *The Political Economy of Slavery*. New York: Pantheon Books.

————. 1968. *In Red and Black*. New York: Pantheon.

————. 1969. *The World Slaveholders Made*. New York: Pantheon.

Giardina, Denise. 1987. *Storming Heavens*. New York: Ivey Books.

Gibson, Rex. 1986. *Critical Theory and Education*. London: Hodder and Stroughton.

Giroux, Henry. 1981. *Ideology, Culture, and the Process of Schooling*. Philadelphia, PA: Temple University Press.

————. 1983. *Theory and Resistance in Education*. South Hadley, Mass: Bergin and Garvey Publishers.

————. 1988. *Schooling and the Struggle for Public Life: Critical Pedagogy in the Modern Age*. Minneapolis, MN: The University of Minnesota Press.

Giroux, Henry and Peter McLaren. 1989. "Schooling, Cultural Politics, and the Struggle for Democracy." In Henry Giroux and Peter McLaren, eds., *Critical Pedagogy, the State, and Cultural Struggle*. Albany, New York: State University of New York Press.

Giroux, Henry A., William F. Pinar, and Anthony N. Penna. 1981. *Curriculum and Instruction*. Berkeley, CA: McCuthchan Publishing Corporation.

Gouldner, Alvin W. 1976. *The Dialectic of Ideology and Technology*. New York: Oxford University Press.

Gray, Richard. 1986. *Writing the South: Ideas of An American Region*. New York: Cambridge University Press.

Greene, Maxine. 1975. *Teacher as Stranger*. Belmont, CA: Wadsworth.

Grumet, Madeleine. 1988. "Women and Teaching." In W. F. Pinar, ed. *Contemporary Curriculum Discourses*.

Gwin, M. 1985. Green-eyed Monsters of the Slavocracy. In Moijorie Pryre and Hortense J. Spillers, eds., *Black Women, Fiction, and Literary Tradition*. Bloomington, IN: Indiana University Press.

Habermas, Jurgen. 1970. *Knowledge and Human Interests*. Trans. Jeremy Shapiro. London: Heinemann.

Hamphill, W., Schlegel, M., and Engleberg, S. 1957. *Cavalier Commonwealth*. New York: McGraw-Hill.

Harding, Sandra. 1986. *The Science Question in Feminisn*. Ithaca, New York: Cornell University Press.

Harvard, William C. 1981. "The Distinctiveness of the South: Fading or Reviving." In Fifteen Southerners, *Why the South Will Survive*. Athens, GA: University of Georgia Press.

Held, David. 1980. *Introduction to Critical Theory: Horkheimer to Habermas*. Berkeley, CA: University of California Press.

Hobson, Fred. 1981. "A South Too Busy to Hate." In Fifteen Southerners, *Why the South Will Survive*. Athens, GA: University of Georgia Press.

Hoffman, F. J. 1967. *The Art of Southern Fiction*. Carbondale, IL: Southern Illinois University Press.

Huebner, Dwayne. 1975. "Curricular Language and Classroom Meanings." In William F. Pinar, *Curriculum Theorizing: The Reconceptualists*. Berkeley, CA: McCutchan Publishing Corporation.

Jacoby, Russell. 1975. *Social Amnesia. Boston, MA: Beacon Press*.

Jagger, Allison M. 1983. *Feminist Politics and Human Nature*. Totowa, New Jersey: Rowman and Allanheld.

Jasckik, Scott. 1988. Case charging Mississippi had a segregated system of higher education is dismissed by a federal judge. *The Chronicle of Higher Education,* January 6.

Kaplan, Cora. 1986. *Sea Changes: Culture and Feminism.* London: Verso.

Karnig, A. & McClain, P. 1985. The New South and Black Economic and Political Development: Changes From 1970 to 1980. *The Western Political Quarterly,* 38, 539–550.

Katz, A. 1988. Economist: Third World Hurting Sunbelt Growth. *The Times Picayune,* March 25. C–2.

Kincheloe, Joe. 1988. "Social Psychoanalysis: Critical Theory and Historiography." A paper presented to the Southern History of Education Society in Atlanta, Georgia.

King, W. 1979. South Leads the Country in School Desegregation. *The New York Times,* May 9. A 16.

Kovel, Joel. 1981. *The Age of Desire.* New York: Pantheon Books.

Lasch, Christopher. 1984. *The Minimal Self.* New York: Norton.

Lawson, Lewis A. 1984. *Another Generation: Southern Fiction Since World War II.* Jackson, MS: University of Mississippi Press.

Mandle, J.R. 1978. *The Roots of Black Poverty.* Durham, NC: Duke University Press.

Marcuse, Herbert. 1960. *Reason and Revolution: Hegel and the Risk of Social Theory.* Boston, MA: Beacon Press.

———. 1964. *One Dimensional Man.* Boston, MA: Beacon Press.

———. 1978. *The Aesthetic Dimension.* Boston, MA: Beacon Press.

MacKethan, Lucinda Hardwick. 1980. *The Dream of Arcady: Place and Time in Southern Literature.* Baton Rouge, LA: LSU Press.

McCarthy, Thomas. 1978. *The Critical Theory of Jurgen Habermas.* Cambridge, MA: The MIT Press.

McLaren, Peter. 1985. "The Ritual Dimensions of Restance: Clowning and Symbolic Inversion." *Journal of Education,* CLXVII No. 2.

————. 1989. *Life in Schools.* New York: Longman.

Miller, Janet L. 1988. "The Resistance of Women Academics: An Autobiographical Account." In W. F. Pinar, ed. *Contemporary Curriculum Discourses* (pp. 486–494), Scottsdale, AZ: Gorsuch Scarisbrick.

Montgomery, Marion. 1981. "Solzhenitsyn as Southerner." In Fifteen Southerners, *Why the South Will Survive.* Athens, GA: University of Georgia Press.

Moore, J. W. 1981. Minorities in the American Class System. *Daedalus 110,* 275–299.

Moore, R. B. 1980. *Two History Tests: A Study in Contrast.* The Racism and Sexism Resource Center for Educators.

Morris, Willie. 1983a. *Always Stand in Against the Curve.* Oxford, MS: Yoknapatawpha Press.

————. 1983b. *The Courting of Marcus Dupree.* Garden City, New York: Doubleday and Company.

————. 1967. *North Toward Home.* Oxford, MS: Yoknapatawpha Press.

————. 1981. *Terrains of the Heart.* Oxford, MS: Yoknapatawpha Press.

Moyers, Bill. 1981. PBS television special on "Creativity."

Ollman, Bertell. 1986. "The Meaning of Dialectics." *Monthly Review,* 38 (Nov.): 42–55.

O'Neale, Sondra. 1984. "Reconstruction of the Composite Self: New Images of Black Women in Maya Angelou's Continuing Autobiography." In M. Evans, ed. *Black Women Writers 1950–1980: A Critical Evaluation,* 25–36. Garden City, New York: Anchor Press/Doubleday.

Page, Myra. 1977. *Daughter of the Hills: A Woman's Part in the Coal Miners' Struggle.* New York: The Feminist Press.

Percy, Walker. 1971. *Love in the Ruins.* New York: Avon Books.

————. 1977. *Lancelot.* London: Farrar, Straus, and Giroux.

Phillips, Ulrich Bonnell. 1963. *Life and Labor in the Old South.* Boston, MA: Pinar, W. F. (n.d.). "The Corporate Production of Feminism and the Case of Boy George."

Pinar, W. F. 1988. *Contemporary Curriculum Discourses*. Scotts-dale, AR: Gorsuch Scarisbrick.

———. 1988. "Introduction." In Pinar, William F. ed., *Contempo-rary Curriculum Discourses*. Scottsdale, AZ: Gorsuch Scaris-brick Publishers.

———. 1988. " 'Whole, Bright, Deep with Understanding': Issues in Qualitative Research and Autobiographical Method." In his *Contemporary Curriculum Discourses*. Scottsdale, AR: Gorsuch Scarisbrick.

Potter, David. 1969. *The South and the Sectional Conflict*. Baton Rouge, LA: Louisiana State University Press.

Pratt, Minnie Bruce. 1984. "Identity: Skin Blood Heart." In E. Bulkin, M. B. Pratt, and B. Smith, *Yours in Struggle: Three Feminist Perspectives on Anti-Semitism and Racism*. Brook-lyn, New York: Long Haul Press.

Reagan, Charles and William Ferris. 1989. *Encyclopedia of South-ern Culture*. Chapel Hill, NC and London: University of North Carolina Press.

Reed, John Shelton. 1982. *One South: An Ethnic Approach to Re-gional Culture*. Baton Rouge, LA: LSU Press.

Reynolds, Barbara. 1988. "Maya Angelou: One of Contemporary Literature's Great Voices Has Seen Life From Many Angles." *Shreveport Times*, (Sun., Jan. 31): 1E–2E.

Roland, Charles. 1982. "The Ever-vanishing South." *The Journal of Southern History 48*, 3–20.

Schubert, W. H. 1986. *Curriculum: Perspective, Paradign, and Pos-sibility*. New York: Macmillian.

Sellers, C. G. 1960. *The Southerner as American*. Chapel Hill, NC: The University of North Carolina Press.

Sentelle, David B. 1981. "Listen and Remember." In Fifteen South-erners, *Why the South Will Survive*. Athens, GA: University of Georgia Press.

Shaker, Paul and Kridel, Craig. 1989. "The Return to Experience: A Reconceptualist Call." *Teacher Education* (January-February).

Simpson, Lewis. 1983. *The Dispossessed Garden*. Baton Rouge, LA and London: Louisiana State University Press.

Smith, Lee. 1980. *Black Mountain Breakdown*. New York: Ballantine Books.

————. 1983. *Oral History*. New York: Ballantine Books.

Still, James. 1978. *River of Earth*. 1934. Reprint. Lexington, KY: University of Kentucky Press.

Styron, William. 1980. *Sophie's Choice*. New York: Bantam Books.

Urban Appalachian Council Fact Sheet. 1985. Cincinnati: Urban Appalachian Council.

Urban, Wayne J. 1981. "History of Education: A Southern Exposure." *History of Education Quarterly 21,* 131–45.

Walker, Alice. 1983. "The Black Writer and the Southern Experience." In her, *In Search of Our Mothers' Gardens*. New York: Harcourt Brace Jovanovich.

Weaver, Richard. 1968. *The Southern Tradition at Bay*. New Rochelle, New York: Arlington House.

Welty, Eudora. 1977. "Place in Fiction." In Eudora Welty, *The Eye of the Story*. New York: Random House.

Whitson, James Anthony. 1988. "The Politics of the 'Non-political' Curriculum." In W. F. Pinar, ed., *Contemporary Curriculum Discourses*. Scottsdale, AZ: Gorsuch Scarisbrick.

Wilmore, Gayroud S. 1983. *Black Religion and Black Radicalism*. Mary Knoll, N.Y.: Orbis.

Wilson, Clyde N. 1981. "Introduction: Should the South Survive?" In Fifteen Southerners, *Why the South Will Survive*. Athens, GA: University of Georgia Press.

Wilson, Charles Reagen and William Ferris, eds. 1989. *Encyclopedia of Southern Culture,* Chapel Hill, NC and London: University of North Carolina Press.

Winkler, K. J. 1988. "Scholars Extend Definition of Southern Culture by Including History of Blacks, Ethnic Groups." *The Chronicle of Higher Education,* January 27. p. A–8.

Woodward, C. Vann. 1968. *The Burden of Southern History.* Baton Rouge, LA: Louisiana State University Press.

Yoder, Edwin M. 1967. "Introduction." In Willie Morris, *North Toward Home.* Oxford, MS: Yoknapatawpha Press.

Zinn, Howard. 1984. "What is Radical History?" In Robert R. Sherman, ed. *Understanding History of Education.* Cambridge, MA: Schenkman Publishing Company.

Contributors

Clinton B. Allison is Professor of Education in History of Education, University of Tennessee, Knoxville. He is an expert in the history of southern education, having published numerous articles on the topic.

Kathleen P. Bennett is Assistant Professor of Education in Anthropology of Education, University of Tennessee, Knoxville. Her work in educational anthropology has often focused on Native American education in Alaska. She recently published (with Margaret D. LeCompte) *How Schools Work: A Sociological Analysis of Education* (Longman).

Louis A. Castenell, Jr. is Dean of the College of Education, University of Cincinnati. A student of race and education, he is co-editing a book with William Pinar entitled, *African-American Education: Issues of History, Gender, and Politics.*

Susan Huddleston Edgerton is a doctoral student in curriculum theory at Louisiana State University, Baton Rouge. She has published several articles on autobiography, feminist theory, and science education in a political and gender context.

Joe L. Kincheloe is Professor of Education, Clemson University. He has written numerous articles on southern educational history and recently published books entitled, *Getting Beyond the Facts: Social Studies Education in the Late Twentieth Century* (Lang) and *Teachers as Researchers: Qualitative Paths to Teacher Empowerment* (Falmer).

Joseph Newman is Professor of Education, University of South Alabama in Mobile. He is a well-respected student of southern eduational history. His *America's Teachers: An Introduction to Education* (Longman) is regarded as an excellent undergraduate social foundations text.

William F. Pinar is Chair of the Department of Curriculum and Instruction, Louisiana State University, Baton Rouge. He has written numerous articles and books in curriculum theory and is recognized as an important figure in the struggle to reshape the curriculum field.

Name Index

223

Subject Index

227